Burning CDs

Eric Charton

GW00702706

An imprint of PEARSON EDUCATION

PEARSON EDUCATION LIMITED

Head Office:
Edinburgh Gate
Harlow
Essex CM20 2JE
Tel: +44 (0) 1279 623623
Fax: +44 (0) 1279 431059

London Office:
128 Long Acre
London WC2E 9AN
Tel: +44 (0) 171 447 2000
Fax: +44 (0) 171 240 5771

_____

First published in Great Britain 2000

© Pearson Education Limited 2000

First published in 1999 as
Se Former En Un Jour: Gravure des CD
by CampusPress France
19, rue Michel Le Comte
75003 Paris
France

Library of Congress Cataloging in Publication Data
Available from the publisher.

British Library Cataloguing in Publication Data
A CIP catalogue record for this book can be obtained from the British Library.

ISBN 0-13-086444-7

10   9   8   7   6   5   4   3   2   1

Translated and typeset by Cybertechnics, Sheffield.
Printed and bound in Great Britain by Ashford Colour Press, Gosport, Hampshire.

The publishers' policy is to use paper manufactured from sustainable forests.

Contents

■■

Introduction

■■

A whole book to learn how to write a CD? How useful is it going to be? CD writing is easy and doesn't cost a lot, you just 'plug', you 'play', you click, and Bob's your uncle! At least this is what some people would have you believe, starting with manufacturers and publishers, and not forgetting the distributors, who are over the moon at the prospect of a highly lucrative market in private CD reproduction!

But stop right there! By bringing prices down dramatically for CD writers and all their accessories (such as CD-Rs, software), manufacturers and publishers may have given you a poisoned gift! True, installing CD writing equipment is not very complicated, and, yes, the software is user friendly and fairly clever; but in practice, anyone wanting to duplicate a CD will need a solid technical background to be able to achieve sensible results.

Because the CD writer is not a simple piece of equipment: its technology is as reliable as it is sophisticated. An extremely accurate laser, which prints 600 tracks per millimetre, using the chemical properties of a multilayered polymer disk, is not something to be taken lightly, even if it has cost a few hundred Euros...

The outcome? Recurrent problems when attempting to burn a CD, which are usually impossible for a beginner to solve. Universal CDs, at least on the face of it, which in practice come in multitudes of formats! This happy free-for-all situation should not really affect users, but, unfortunately for them, it does become a veritable puzzle!

So, these are the problems connected with writing a CD-R (CD Recordable), summarised in a few paragraphs. Which explains why we are now going to be writing here, on paper, the essential items of information that you, dear reader, will need if you want to be able to write easily and quickly whatever it is that you wish to write on to your CD-Rs.

Is this possible? Of course, just follow the laser!

■ What you'll find in this book

During the first part, which will take up three chapters, we will explain the theory behind CD writing. The first chapter to learn about the concept of CD-R (CD Recordable), a second chapter to discover the rules, from CD-I (Compact Disk Interactive) to CD-ROM (Compact Disk Read Only Media) via the video CD.

The third chapter will describe how a CD-R works and will introduce some equipment which is currently on the market. This is essential: you'll be able to sort out things which go wrong only if you are fully aware of how the equipment works.

A few more chapters and you'll be able to transform the new box of sophisticated equipment you have just bought into a working CD recording station: Chapters 4 and 5 are, in fact, dedicated to installing your equipment.

If you think you are already familiar with CD burning and its rules, you are probably thinking that you can save yourself some time. This can work out perfectly: the practical sections start with Chapter 6. Study it carefully! You may find it so interesting that you may be late for the following chapters, where we will explain how to record anything, from video CDs to karaoke CDs, via CD-ROMs and video games CDs...

Time flies, and you are now getting to the operational stage: from Chapter 7 to Chapter 10, you'll practise how to write a CD, step by step, application by application. The last of these four chapters is dedicated to troubleshooting problems you may have come across.

In Chapter 11, you'll actually produce a beautiful CD-R, ready to go. In Chapter 12, we will prepare you for what you are likely to read tomorrow morning: how to burn a DVD, how much it costs and what it's for.

And finally, you'll have finished with this book, and you can then go to bed, go out clubbing, have dinner in a restaurant, in short, you can then wander off to one of the thousands of occupations which keep you away from your PC, at least for a while. Burning and copying CDs is certainly wonderful, but don't overdo it!

■ The new edition...

Just a few last words, before getting down to it, on this new edition, updated and corrected. The first version of this book came out in 1998. Just one year... sufficient to revolutionise the CD burning market however.

So what's happened in this year that's so important? Tons of changes! Judge for yourself:

- The average speed of CD writers has gone from 1×/2× to 2×/4×.

- The average price of CD writers has dropped from £250–350 to less than £150.

- The Easy CD Creator software, which up to very recently was the only CD writing software on the market, is now facing strong competition from a variety of (excellent) new products.

- The IDE writer, previously badly used by PCs, is now as good as the SCSI one, and costs much less.
- According to the current shared wisdom, the CD-RW (re-writable CD) function is almost a standard.
- The 'audio extraction' function, which allows audio disks to be copied has now become a standard on all CD writers and will soon be the same on CD readers.

In the light of these changes, which have revolutionised the market, we are entitled to ask the question: 'What else is going to happen this year?' and, as a consequence: 'How are CDs going to be written in the next century (just a few months away from the day I am writing these lines)?' We already have the overall development picture:

- progressive increase of standard writing speed to 4×then to 6× and then to 8× (end of 1999);
- systematic use of the CD-RW function (this is almost the case now), which should finally replace diskettes;
- fast decrease in price to less than £100 for average CD writers (end of 1999);
- integration of the CD-RW function (1999? 2000?) in Windows 98 with the OSTA UDF norm;
- CD-RW prices coming down from £10 – which is what they cost currently – to less than £5 (1999? 2000?);
- CD-R aluminium disks (cheaper than gold) down to 50p (1999? 2000?).

These are not just empty prophecies: all manufacturers have already come out with 6x or 8x speed CD writers – all CD-RW. CD writers which cost less than £100 already exist. I cannot really check the information on integration of the CD-RW function in a Windows 98 upgrade (and as standard in Windows 2000?), which anyway I got through the grapevine. But all the emerging technologies and the ones that are fast becoming the standard (CD-ROM, cable transfer, antivirus) have been integrated quickly and without charge to the user within the Microsoft system. The way the market is going for CD recorders, we are entitled to believe that Microsoft will shortly integrate most 'CD burning' functions in Windows.

A shifting market, a disappearing diskette!

It's an established fact: the CD writers market is shifting! Most important, the equipment has become truly democratic, actually accessible to anyone, not only because of the price but also because its software is so simple and user-friendly. Which makes me repeat what I was saying before, that the CD-RW function should now be quickly integrated into Windows to replace diskette drives in the middle term, which to my mind is going to happen anyway. Media at a small price, 600 MB available for storage, perfectly acceptable data access time (compared with a diskette drive) and easy installation of ever bigger compatible CD-RW writers: ideal conditions for such a development.

■ What do I read after this book?

The logical follow up to this book, in the same series, should be a book on audio CD. This is a subject that I personally believe should be developed because it interests so many readers (actually, possibly the same number of readers may be interested in duplicating video games CDs, but, hey, a book on that subject...).

If you want to take the subject further, there is also a much bigger book, very comprehensive, aimed at more expert users: *CD Burning* published by Macmillan. It covers all the practical and technical issues touched on in my book, but it takes them much further. A second book on the same subject (which covers the same area as the first part of the Macmillan title) has also been published, with a CD-ROM containing the main demo versions for software currently available: its title is *Starting CD burning.*

■ Some basic questions and their answers

Q How is data recorded on a CD-R?

Answer in Chapter 3.

Q What is XA? CD-PLUS? Mode 1? A Photo-CD?

Answer in Chapter 1.

Q What is the lifespan of a CD-R?

Answer in Chapter 2.

Q What's the purpose of CD books such as *Red Book*, *Green Book*, and so on?

Answer in Chapter 1.

Q How long does it take to burn a CD?

Answer in Chapter 3.

Q How do you copy a CD-I, a video CD, an audio CD?

Answer in Chapter 6.

■ Special icons

As well as text and diagrams in this book you'll find special entries that underline certain specific points.

 Under this heading, you will find additional information.

This symbol warns you about problems that may arise in certain circumstances. It also warns what not to do. If you follow the instructions, you should not have any problems.

 This symbol provides you with suggestions and tips: keyboard shortcuts, advanced techniqes, and so on.

1
Important background information on CD recording

The first chapter gives some background theory about the media. What actually is a CD writer? And is the CD it produces a real CD? What are the things to do and not to do, how to assess the potential of CD-Rs?

■ From CD-ROM to CD-R

The first step is to understand the difference between CD-ROMs (and more generally, CDs in all their aspects, audio disks, multimedia disks...) and CD-Rs. CD-ROMs and audio CDs, such as the ones you buy in shops, are very different from the disks you'll be using with a CD writer.

At the beginning, nobody had really thought of the possibility of reading a CD (which would become a CD-ROM) on a PC, even less of the possibility of burning your own CD!

The main feature of 'commercial' CDs is that they have been produced industrially. They compare to CD-Rs the same way as a photocopied document compares to a printed book. They are manufactured from a very sophisticated mould called 'glass master'.

Brief reminder: the CD standard was invented by two companies, Sony and Philips. It was inspired by the manufacturers' need to replace vinyls with better quality media: at the time, the buzzword was 'digital'. The standard was therefore set, contained in a book produced jointly by the two companies: the *Red Book*. We will deal with this in Chapter 2. With this first norm, it was simply a question of being able to enjoy better sound in a your living-room.

Explanations: the two electronic giants, who were, above all, manufacturers of hi-fi equipment and for whom disk production was a secondary activity (Philips' associate company Polygram for example), hoped, by introducing a new standard, to get round the practice of vinyl disks being copied on to audio-cassettes. And also, this meant that consumers had to purchase new disk players...

With the CD, you could enjoy digital quality, which means the same quality as the original recording, a quality which up to then could not be achieved with a cassette. You could therefore entice music lovers to renew their library and, most of all, and this is the clever bit, discourage them from copying on to their cassettes by getting their ears attuned to better sound quality!

However, digital means binary, and binary means computer!

Introduction to the binary system

The binary system is the basic language for all computers. It starts from the concept that everything can be coded using electronic switches: switched off (0) or switched on (1). If you put together a set of 0s and 1s (that is, the bits), you get a combination. Eight bits, for example, make up a byte, providing 256 possible combinations. The binary system can represent everything: sound, images, text. That is how your computer works.

And so the *Yellow Book* came out, as a logical follow up to the *Red Book*, which specifies how a CD can become a CD-ROM by replacing audio-digital data with compressed digital data, associated to a file management system. Digital data, file system: All that is left is to connect up to a PC or a Mac. This is the CD-ROM reader, whose electronic and mechanical set up is virtually the same as for your domestic audio CD player, with a sprinkle of computer components on top.

We are not yet talking about copying: we are only talking about reading a CD-ROM on computer. All publishers were over the moon: to manufacture a CD-ROM, you needed industrial equipment to which the public at large does not have access. If you were to store over 100 MB of data on this medium, it would be impossible to copy the software on to a diskette or hard disk because it would be too big (at the time a hard disk was rarely bigger than 300 MB). Illegal copying of software – particularly video games – would therefore be over.

Then one company noted that the market for a CD copier could be a very juicy one, especially since CD-ROM capacity (500 to 600 MB), huge at the time, was gradually becoming commonplace: hard disks were reaching gigabytes and backup systems were about to be capable of transferring the total contents of a CD within minutes.

They then came up with the CD-R, *CD Recordable*, by writing the *Orange Book*. Only a few people realised at the time that this new standard would bring a revolution to the market. With a domestic writer, sitting on the user's desktop, you could now achieve the same results as the best equipped music producers or publishers of multimedia-based encyclopaedias.

To achieve this prowess, CD-R media is very different from CDs or CD-ROMs. Sold blank, it's designed to be written (burnt) when the CD is of course unwritable. We will see that its physical properties and the material it's made of are very sophisticated. However, thanks to the *Orange Book*, the CD-R, so different from a CD, can be read by any CD-ROM or audio CD reader.

Obviously, at the beginning, the very high cost of CD burners (about £3000, then £1500, then £500) inhibited their diffusion. But everybody knows that in the magic world of computers, for years now a small fairy has made it its business to trample on prices continually and with all the delicacy of an elephant!

It's difficult to tell just how low prices of CD writers will go. If we look at developments for PC prices, even those of CD-ROM drives, we might assume that in a couple of years we

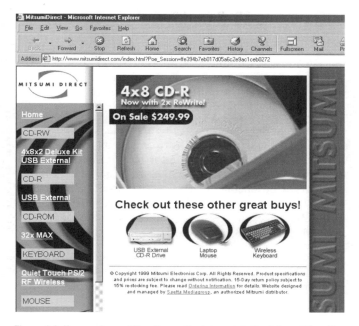

Figure 1.1 You can buy a CD writer on the Internet; in the future, PCs will probably come with a CD writer as standard.

will be buying PCs no longer equipped with CD 24× readers, but with write-readers! We can imagine that for £50, in a few years, everybody will be able to burn a CD-R at the flip of a switch, thanks to standard software included with Windows 2000! (It's interesting that Microsoft has called its software for the year 2000 Windows 2000 rather than Windows 0.)

CD writers are not the only things that have come down in price: CD-Rs, up to now sold at a crazy price (because apparently they are gold plated), have seen their price tumble. Now less than £1, will they soon fall to 20p or 30p (which is what they are in the USA)? Who knows...

▪ How does a CD-R work?

The scene is set: from now on CD-R and CD-ROM will use the same drive. We now need to understand how it works. The best thing is to go through the mysteries of their technology and study how both are manufactured.

The two technologies CD-R and 'industrial' CD, have in common that they both create alternate 'pits' and 'bumps' on the disk. These pits and bumps are created on a support disk, covered with a metal layer, with the lot sandwiched between two bits of transparent plastic. It's the metal layer with the pits that, by producing different refractions of light issued by a laser beam, allows data to be read. Transformed by the CD drive electronics into sets of 0s and 1s, the data, once assembled, make up bits of music, programs and files.

The same way of working then for both media: this explains why a CD reader can read both a CD-ROM and a CD-R. So what are the differences? The manufacturing process:

- Commercial CDs are burnt in large batches in an industrial process. They are manufactured by moulding a master on a plastic layer. Then, this layer is sandwiched with an aluminium sheet between two wafers of translucent substance, and the whole is brought together and moulded under pressure. The last stage is the application of a screen print by a traditional printing process.

- CD-Rs, on the other hand, cannot be pressed mechanically. They are made with an office writer using a laser. The laser strips colour from the surface of the disk, creating 'pits' and 'bumps'. After the treatment with the laser, the parts which had been burnt by the laser in the writer no longer reflect light, and generate the same effect as an industrial CD on the laser of a CD-ROM reader.

The functioning principle of a CD-ROM reader's laser

The optical mechanism of a CD-ROM reader is sensitive to the presence or absence of light generated by the impact of a laser beam on the medium. Lack of light corresponds to a pit (which causes the laser beam to deviate), while a bump produces presence of light by reflection.

First note: the CD-R writer 'burns' the medium. And when you say burning, you mean for ever. The main feature of CD writers is that they can only write once to a single location.

What can we deduce from this? That the first system is ideal for large runs (at least one thousand), because it's fast, reliable and cheap.

That the second system, the CD-R, is much slower, slightly less reliable, much more expensive, but it's a must for one-off production or for prototypes for short runs.

Summing up, the advantages and the disadvantages of the industrial CD are:

- the low cost for large runs (less than 20p each over three thousand);
- the possibility of creating printed CDs;
- speed (a few hours for several thousand disks);
- it's impossible to test and experiment with the CD: the 'glass master' costs from £400 to £1,000.

On the other hand, the advantages and the disadvantages of the CD-R are:

- the single CD has an unbeatable price;
- experimenting with a project is very simple;
- the system is user-friendly, for small runs (less than 30);
- printing a good quality label is difficult;

■ the unit cost is high (80p, plus the cost of the time spent and of equipment wear and tear).

The scene is set, now let's explore the secret paths of the media!

■ Relevant facts on the CD-R

The CD-R, because of its history, has some peculiarities. The first and most important one: CD-Rs are in practice 'a product' derived from the first audio CD. This historical fact explains why even today we refer to 'sound recording capacity', and not 'capacity in megabytes'.

This does not make any difference whatsoever as far as you are concerned. In effect, sound tracks in audio disks are burnt in the same way as for a hard disk, with a sequence of 0s and 1s. As a result, to calculate the capacity of a CD-R, simply translate the number of bits corresponding to n recording minutes as the number of bytes which can be reserved for programs.

Commercial CD-Rs that you find in shops are sold in two versions, with 63 and 74 recording minutes. This corresponds to 550 MB or 650 MB respectively.

How to calculate the capacity of a CD-R

Because of their audio origin, CDs are quantified in minutes: seconds:sectors. Each second contains 75 sectors. Any sector may contain 2,048 bytes (2 KB). A 63-minute CD-R can therefore be calculated according to the following formula:

63 minutes × (60 seconds) × (75 sectors) × (2 KB) = 567,000 KB, where 1 MB equals 1,024 KB: 567,000 / 1,024 = 553 MB.

Careful, this formula only applies to CD writing in mode 2 (see standards later). Other standards include bytes reserved for error correction and therefore reduce the available space.

If they have the same capacity, do CD-Rs also have the same composition? Not at all! They differ by their 'coating' which affects their lifespan (from 10 to 100 years). A CD-R has a polycarbonate base layer. This layer is burnt in a spiral track, 'pre-structured', which takes up the whole of its surface. This is used to guide the laser beam during the burning process. This layer is covered with a second layer, translucent, which may be made of different types of substance (in some more expensive cases CD-Rs may even be covered in glass). The whole thing is then covered with a reflective layer, often in gold (a very thin layer, between 50 and 100 nm!), occasionally in silver. The top layer, which covers the whole lot, is plastic. This is the layer where labels can be printed with a silk screen technique.

Look and learn

You'll note, by looking at several CD-Rs from different manufacturers, that they are not all the same colour. It's the reflective surface which gives the CD its colour. Green ones have a reflective top layer in gold, while grey ones are usually in silver. The typical colour of these metals distinguishes CD-Rs from 'industrial' disks, whose reflective layer is usually of aluminium. If you look at a CD-R against an illuminated electric light bulb, you'll find that the reflective layer is so thin that you can see through it!

Figure 1.2 The CD-R.

■ Quality of CD-Rs

After discussing their composition, we are now going to discuss quality and lifespan! How good is a CD-R? Is its quality the same as an industrial CD? Will it have a lifespan of 10, 100, 200 years? Is the recording quality the same for a CD that costs 80p (standard price, nowadays) as for a £4 CD? Lots of questions, but no easy answers!

First part of the reply: as in the case of PC memory, only a few manufacturers share the CD-R market, left to market their media under various brand names. The main ones are Kodak, Verbatim, Maxell and TDK. When you buy a disk in an empty box, without a label or the manufacturer's name, from a supermarket or such similar place, you can be sure that it's one of these companies that manufactured it!

Is a 74-minute CD-R not as good as a 63-minute CD?

Up to a few months ago, it was certainly true that longer duration CDs were in general not as good as the shorter ones.

But now, the technology of CD writers and CDs has improved considerably and there is no longer any difference. But an older second-hand CD writer may have some problems with a CD-R longer than 63 minutes.

CD-R manufacturers do not simply manufacture one single type of CD. Some use different substrates, various materials. Occasionally, the manufacturing process is not properly checked and a few thousand CDs fails to meet the requirements of the internal quality control. Do we throw these disks away? No, we sell them! This is where you get your unmarked disks: from a famous manufacturer who does not think they are good enough to be given his own name. This does not necessarily mean that unbranded CDs are not usable, you simply risk a higher failure rate when burning.

As for the big-name CDs, you should note that the manufacturers are at war on the subject of quality! Each swears by his own technology and raw materials, because the data layers may be made of several different materials. The most frequently used are cyanine and phthalocyanine. Cyanine can also be found under several forms 'Raw Cyanine'or 'Metal Stabilized Cyanine'.

TDK, for example, has carried out some very stringent tests on these two types of material. The manufacturer has come to the conclusion that 'raw cyanine is not at all suitable for CD-Rs production, because it's too sensitive to light'. Adding 'one single exposition to a xenon light would be enough to fracture the molecular structure of the CD, rendering it useless'. Obviously, TDK disks use 'Metal Stabilized Cyanine'...

Some manufacturers have solved the problem by switching to a different type of material, phthalocyanine, invented by Mitsumi, who then sold it under licence to other manufacturers.

The intervention of the ANSI committee

The ANSI IT9 committee is currently trying to establish a test method for determining the lifespan of CD-ROMs and CD-Rs. The manufacturers have all tried to establish their own test protocols and mathematical modes to evaluate the precise lifespans of these media. Unhappily, their conclusions vary between 70 and 200 years! An ANSI standard test protocol would allow a more precise evaluation (source MAXELL).

■ What is the lifespan of a CD-R?

Finally, let's evaluate the lifespan of a CD-R. Let's say that, for 90% of users, it's sufficient! Your files, your applications and your data will be safe for at least 50 years on this media, regardless of origin, which should suffice for a common mortal who will possibly not outlive his archives!

TDK states that its 'Metal Stabilized Cyanine' products, tested under accelerated ageing conditions, could be guaranteed for 70 years.

A peal from another bell. In a document published by the Eastman Kodak company in 1995, the authors Douglas Stinson, Fred Ameli and Nick Zaino gave as their opinion on the lifespan of CD-Rs: 'We foresee that the lifespan of the Kodak photo-CD and CD-Rs, under normal storage conditions, at home or in the office, could reach 100 years, and perhaps more.'

That is Kodak's official stance on this subject. But the researchers did not stop there, they did not hesitate to add that, 'in their view, Kodak's official position is a pessimistic interpretation (a praiseworthy attitude for the NDLA consumer) of their own research'. According to them, under normal conditions of wear and tear, the most optimistic estimate of the potential lifespan of a CD-R could be given as 217 years. They went on to add: 'Everything depends on what can be regarded as normal conditions of storage'!

Why spend so much time trying to evaluate the lifespan of a CD-R? Because these new media can be used to store documents of capital importance. Business records, accounts data, and other numerical information. Musical composers are more concerned on this subject than anyone: one sees how difficult it is to renovate sound archives from the beginning of the century, recorded in microgrooves. If these restored sound archives (nearly always transferred on to CD-R nowadays) should be lost after only a few years, you can imagine the cost – we will return to this subject.

Meanwhile, let's talk about us. What is our preoccupation? Let's say, for naïve burners such as us, that the longevity of CD-Rs imposes the following constraints:

- a disk exposed to light and heat will have its lifespan reduced.

- a poor quality disk is more sensitive to heat and light;

- it's not reasonable to expect a duration of more than 50 years for data stored on a CD-R;

and forces us therefore to apply the following precepts:

- it's preferable to store CD-Rs for archive purposes in zones of medium and constant temperature;

- it's preferable not to store these CDs where they are exposed to direct light;

- important data or archives which you hope will endure should definitely be stored only on CD-Rs of good quality;

- bargain or unbranded CDs should be reserved for data with a survival priority of 10 years at the most.

So far as I am concerned, dear reader, I have a small advantage over you. My book is recorded at the Bibliothèque Nationale (in France, where it's the law...) which spends millions (hundreds of millions?) of francs to ensure that my work will survive down the centuries. My posterity is therefore assured, no need of a CD-R for this book!

An author of importance will have even more chance than myself: his book will be burnt on a glass CD-R. This is very fine, it's expensive, and apparently is guaranteed for 500 years!

■ What type of information can a CD hold?

That said, the CD-R writer installed on your PC is not limited only to the recording and archiving of information data. That is the most elementary of its functions. The CD-R, because it's a media, that is to say an information carrier, is capable of holding almost anything that a CD can hold. Films, photos, multimedia applications or even audio data.

Once burnt, the CD-R is readable like a commercial CD.

It can be used on the audio CD player of your hi-fi system, if you have recorded music; on your domestic CD-I player, if you have burnt a multimedia application compatible to this format; or again, on a Photo-CD viewer if you have recorded photographs in Kodak format.

Again, nothing is stopping you from burning a disk for a Macintosh on your PC, and *vice versa*. As you may already know, many games created for CD reading consoles were themselves burnt, in the first instance, on a PC! You'll read later that they also are reproducible, under certain conditions!

The burner is therefore a tool and the CD-R disk a media that suitable software burner applications can exploit. Its manipulation will create a disk compatible with one of the multiple disk readers on the market. This offers us quite seductive prospects:

- commercial software packages will allow us to create a multimedia disk while inventing an application on a hard disk which we then burn;

- the CD-R writer will produce or reproduce almost all possible forms of audio CD, and these then will be readable on any CD player;

- images will be saved and referenced on CD-R under all possible formats imaginable, as on a Kodak Photo-CD;

- files will be stored in all formats: therefore the contents of a hard disk can be better saved on a CD-R than on a magnetic storage medium.

Figure 1.3 Easy CD-Pro.

The software package is indispensable

It's the burner software, here, Easy CD-Pro, which determines the reproduction capabilities of the burner. On its own, the burner can do nothing. With appropriate software, it's theoretically capable of copying anything, without exception.

2 CD standards

You might think, given the apparent simplicity of burners and software, that you need only click and write. Nothing of the kind! Certainly, it's a single-media CD-R, but it can accept data in a multitude of diverse and varied formats. These are the CD standard formats.

They have been invented to suit the evolution of the market and the needs of users. Of what use are these standards? First and foremost, to send expected data to a peripheral read-unit in a format acceptable to it. This is what standards are for. It's this which will avoid you having to buy a different type of CD-ROM depending on whether you use an *x* or *y* reader.

In a few words, we can describe these standard formats in the following way:

- The domestic audio CD player expects that you give it to read a CD containing musical files, that this data should be specially 'formatted' for it. This is a leading standard defined by the *Red Book*.

- When Windows operates a CD-ROM reader, it expects that this might transmit program data, or files, or even sound sequences. This is another standard contained in another book, the *Yellow Book*.

- Your CD-writer expects that you'll supply it with blank CDs to burn, and it will use appropriate techniques when writing data to disk. Such standard engineering practices are set out in a new book, the *Orange Book*.

These standards are termed backwards-compatible, which means that the most recent standard can, without exception, meet all the formats set by previous standards:

- Your audio CD player will therefore be unable to read a CD-ROM disk.

- The CD-ROM drive on your PC, on the other hand, can decipher both sound and data (in the *Yellow Book* format), because the *Yellow Book* provides backwards compatibility with the *Red Book*.

What can you deduce from all this? That you should certainly differentiate between the software and hardware aspects. CD-R media is capable of recording everything. Your CD-writer, in theory, is capable of writing everything:

- CD-ROMs
- audio CDs
- video CDs
- perhaps even CD-Is or disks for consoles!

It's the software that you use which allows you to write in one or the other of these standard formats.

■ The software standard for CD-R media

Let's then begin with the software standard common to all CD-Rs, and which also applies to industry CDs. By this we mean the tracks 'system', already inscribed when you buy the media. The format of the CD has not changed since the appearance of the DVD. Its software specification (that is, its basic formatting) amounts to a spiral track of 22,188 turns, giving approximately 600 turns per millimetre. To give you an idea of the size this represents, if we unrolled the spiral this would give a straight line of around 6 km in length.

This is the main thing about the principal media material: all CDs correspond absolutely to this format! To give an idea of the technical stability which this consistency represents, imagine that during the same time, the 'low-level' tracks on a 3.5 in. hard disk, which are the the equivalent of those of the CD-R, have had to be modified at least fifty times!

From CD to DVD

The 'CD' hardware support has always observed the same physical format since its creation. Only the DVD, which retains the same dimensions, uses a different system for data organisation.

■ History of software standards and coloured books...

As far as media is concerned then, there is nothing to fear as regards compatibility, no more than faults, at the time of purchase. The CD-R is universal. But things are not quite the same other than where the organisation of written data is concerned. A multitude of standards and formats for writing data is going to affect the future compatibility of your CD.

We have seen that all the standards are set down in 'books'. These are, in part, the standards set by the inventors of the CD. We list them here.

Red Book

The *Red Book* describes the physical format of audio CDs, as well as a simple logical file structure: the sound coded in Digital Audio format. Put simply, it's the format of all commercial Digital Audio CDs for audio CD players.

Yellow Book

The *Yellow Book* describes the physical format of CD-ROM disks before data are inscribed, as well as their logical arrangement. Here is defined the CD-ROM drives mass produced by the industry. The majority of commercial CD-ROM drives follow *Yellow Book* standards.

Green Book

This standard was conceived by Philips to write video on to CDs in a digital form. It describes the format for its CD-I disks (multimedia CDs which work with proprietary CD players). The *Green Book* is very similar to the *Yellow Book*. Disks written to this standard are also readable on a PC, but not workable (the programs contained are intended for Motorola processors).

Orange Book

The *Orange Book*, paradoxically, is the one which is of least interest to us, but which today permits us to write CDs directly on our PCs. It describes the standard and the physical format of CD-Rs. The 'book' is divided into three parts:

- Part I: CD-MO (*Magneto-Optical*)

- Part II: CD-WO (*Write-Once*, that is, any CD capable of being written to only once, including Photo-CD and CD-R disks).

- Part III: CD-RW (*ReWritable*). This covers the CD-drives which should soon appear in the shops, using re-writable CDs. These are the CD-RW ReWrite drives compatible with the majority of current commercial writers.

White Book

The *White Book* describes the format of Video CD-drives. This book includes the characteristics of the *Yellow Book* and of the *Green Book*, to which some definitions of video format are added. *White Book* disks are themselves also readable by CD-ROM drives.

Blue Book

The last of these works on the description of standards, the *Blue Book* describes the CD-Extra format. This format, still rather unknown although mooted in 1995, is a kind of fusion of the audio CD drive and the CD-ROM drive.

How to recognise the contents of a disk by looking at it

All disks corresponding to the different books include a distinctive printed logo: a CD-ROM has a logo 'Compact Disc Data Storage', a CD-video disk 'Compact Disc Digital Video', and audio disk 'Compact Disc Digital Audio', and so on.

■ ...and of the CD-ROM drives that use them

All these books are intended both for manufacturers of hardware (CD read or write units), and for authors of software (who want to create CDs compatible with specific read units). It's for this reason that the *Orange Book*, which defines CD-Write units and the technology of CD-Rs, does not truly concern us: it serves in the manufacture of the hardware which we are going to use to make our disks! On the other hand, the *Yellow Book*, the *Red Book* are essential to us: by using their standards we will be able to write audio-CDs (containing music) or CD-ROM disks.

Differentiate between books and standards

The books define the physical organisation of data on CDs. The standards are 'logical methods' relevant to the organisation or compatibility of data.

The ISO standard 9660, for example, is a standard for logical file format and file structure (a method of description), written on the physical disk tracks compatible to Yellow Book or to Green Book, like the same brand of hard disk can be utilised in a PC or in a Mac, without software on the two machines being compatible.

CD-Extra

A CD on which two sessions are written: the first containing audio data, the second digital data. We will return later to the concept of sessions.

CD-ROM, CD-ROM XA and modes

The CD-ROM is that described by the *Yellow Book*. It can be written in Mode 1. The CD-ROM XA is a CD with extended architecture, that is, intermediate between the CD of the *Yellow Book* and that of the *Green Book*. Defined by Philips and Sony in 1988, this standard allows CD players which support it to synchronise sound and data (the programs) recorded on the disk. The CD-ROM XA can be written in Mode 1 or 2.

Mode 1

- A CD-ROM in Mode 1 comprises sectors of 2,048 bytes that respond to standards set out in the *Yellow Book*.

- FORM-1 contains sectors of 2,048 bytes of data, together with an error correction system. Error correction requires an additional 464 bytes, resulting in sectors of 2,512 bytes.

Mode 2

- A CD in Mode 2 responds to two 'models' of organisation, that of Mode 1 (Sector format FORM-1) and that of Mode 2.

- FORM-2 contains sectors of 2,324 bytes, without error correction, intended to hold audio or video data.

Mode 1 was finalised for the first CD-ROMs. The error correction mechanism was designed with the praiseworthy aim of guaranteeing the quality of the programs read by the PC.

In fact, the computer has the peculiarity that a single bad byte received can provoke a malfunction, which is not the case with audio data (defined by the *Red Book*). For audio, a failing byte corresponds to a fraction of a second of distorted sound, inaudible to the common mortal.

Unhappily, the correction mechanism of Mode 1 slows the CD reading rate considerably because of the time lost in transferring and analysing the 464 error correction bytes.

Hence Mode 2 was invented for multimedia PCs and video applications (CD video amongst others), without checking, and is therefore faster when reading sound and video.

Mode 2 also allows program files or data files to be written, it's used more and more instead of Mode 1 to achieve higher application execution speeds. Error correction is of only relative usefulness given the reliability of current CD-ROM drives: it is, in fact, very rare for these drives to change a single byte.

Sessions

A session is a part of the disk composed of tracks in a given format: for example, of sound, or of PC programs. A multi-session disk is organised according to *Red Book* specifications (holding sound readable by an audio CD player), together with a second session holding data organised according to the *Yellow Book*, intended to be read by the CD-ROM drive on a PC.

The principle of the multi-session mode is simple: if you write only 150 MB to a 600 MB disk, then 450 MB space remains free. Logical! We now want to write to the disk again so that we can make full use of its total capacity. This procedure is not without its restrictions: you can only write a new session if your CD-R is not 'finalised' (that is, locked, sealed and rendered unsuitable for further writing). Problem: while the disk is not closed, you cannot read it with every CD drive. The bad management of this mode is largely a fault of CD-ROM drives, although the phenomenon seems to be less of a problem as drives become more and more compatible.

Origin of multi-session mode.

Multi-session mode was developed for Kodak and Photo-CDs. The idea was that a CD-R containing photos, without being full, could be reused to add further photos in a new session. In the event, the idea, technically feasible, has not been commercialised by Kodak laboratories.

Careful! Multi-session mode is made possible by the operating system, which must be capable of recognizing that a disk contains sessions other than the one which was recorded first. Windows 95, for example, is not always capable of reading several sessions recorded on the same CD – it's the CD unit driver which adds this function! To read multiple sessions, you must sometimes therefore install a CD extension program (the SCSI drivers from Corel, for example, can open multiple sessions).

■ About the method of storing files on CDs!

The file system of a data storage medium is the data organisation mechanism which it contains (programs, files, from the .exe to the .doc and the .wav). All hard disks, diskette drives, even external tape storage drives are furnished with a file-handling system. Your CD-ROM drive containing files is no exception to this rule and is organised by a file-handling system, just like a hard disk, with directories arranged in a tree structure, containing further directories or files.

ISO9660

The ISO9660 is one of the standard formats for file organisation. It's often called 'High Sierra' format, from the name of its devisers. ISO9660 limits the length of file names to that which is found on the older versions of Windows or MS-DOS: 8 characters, a dot, an extension of 3 characters (xxxxxxxx.yyy). Note that ISO9660 does not allow special characters ('$', '#') as in MS-DOS: characters are limited strictly to letters and digits. We would add that the depth of subdirectories is limited to eight levels (unlike some other systems that have no limit).

 ***ISO9660 standard file structure* – Yellow Book**

The Yellow Book *states that the data on a CD starts after a pause of two seconds. Which infers that the first two seconds of a CD-R are not available for recording data. This entails lost capacity, according to the formula give in Chapter 1:*

(2s) $\times$ *(75 sectors)* $\times$ *(2 KB) = 300 KB.*

Furthermore, ISO9660 format requires for recording its structure:

- *Main directory file: one sector minimum*
- *Table of paths: two sectors minimum*
- *First volume Lead-In: one sector*
- *Volume Lead-Out: one sector*
- *Reserved for system use: the first 16 sectors*

ISO9660 adapted for MS-DOS

With most recording software, you'll be able to choose between ISO9660 and MS-DOS file structures.

In the case of MS-DOS you'll have the benefit of several supplementary possibilities of the MS-DOS format, namely the possibility of using characters such as '&', '+', '$' in file names, and directories down to more than 8 levels.

The Joliet of Windows 95 and 98

Since the arrival of Windows 95 there is a third possible file
structure, very little utilised yet on CD-ROM: this is the
'Joliet' format (see Figure 2.1). The Windows 95 file system
is in fact much more sophisticated than ISO9660. It allows
names up to 256 characters long for files and folders (for
example, *the text that I sent you.doc* instead of *text.doc*).

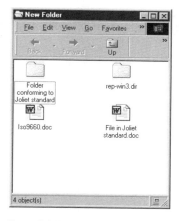

Figure 2.1 The Joliet standard.

Furthermore, to remain compatible with standard DOS
names (a 'Joliet' diskette formatted on a PC running
Windows 95 remains readable on a PC running an older version of DOS or Windows 3.x), the basic form of file names
remains the same thanks to a trick: for file names of more
than 8 characters the 'tilde' symbol (~) is added after the
sixth letter, followed by a number, and the remainder of the
text is stored in a new zone defined by the 'Joliet' format.
Thus, the file name *Letter to send.doc* is broken down into
Letter~1.doc, with the remainder of the name stored afterwards in the form *to send.doc*.

A few details. To make this new name format compatible with the file structures of CD-ROMs, Microsoft has devised a 'Joliet' extension of ISO9660. With this extension, your CD-Rs can contain files with names up to 64 characters in length. These new generation CDs remain, in theory, compatible with the older versions of MS-DOS. The Joliet format is gradually becoming the standard on all PCs (in general equipped with Windows 95 or 98). As a result, therefore, it's becoming standard for CD-Rs. It's still possible to use MS-DOS format to make a disk compatible with Windows 3.x, but for how much longer?

To create a Joliet format CD-ROM, your recording software must simply support that standard. Almost all recent versions of software are capable of it.

Attention! Some versions of Windows NT (3.51 – 1057) cannot read Joliet standard CD-Rs. On the other hand, there is no problem with NT 4.0.

And Romeo!

Standard writers have a sense of humour: no Joliet without Romeo! They have therefore devised a subset of Joliet, universal, permitting file names of 128 characters, including spaces. Romeo files can be read under DOS and Windows 3.1 in the traditional form (eight letters, a dot, a three letter extension) and under Windows 95 and NT 3.51 in their full length. But also, and this is an advantage for Romeo, on Macintosh machines. Note, on these machines Romeo file names are readable... if they are no longer than 31 characters. But you can forget Romeo, it's a standard too far which serves no purpose: it's necessary to apply a patch to bring your system up to date to use it.

Macintosh HFS

HFS format is the file system native to the Macintosh. You can use HFS format to write CDs but, in this case, they will only be compatible with Mac OS based computers. One advantage, you'll preserve the Apple Macintosh 'look', with its typically stylish icons.

OSTA UDF: new diskettes?

Because of its rewrite ability the CD-RW function does not allow the adoption of a standard format file management system: CD-R formatting is intended to be permanent (it's therefore impossible to go back afterwards to erase or modify a directory or a file, for example). Enough said! Mass storage formats (FAT 32 in Windows 98 for example) are designed for magnetic recording devices. Probably they could have been adapted for the CD-RW drive but it seems that Microsoft did not wish it. In short, the standard file format for these disks is the OSTA UDF! How does it work? You use specific software (Direct CD for example) to format the CD-RW like a hard disk, then, by installing a driver to read OSTA UDF format, you have access to your disk in Windows Explorer. You can copy or move any item just as on a hard disk.

Other standards

There are three other types of CD organisation which are available: Rock Ridge which is used by Unix systems to store long file names, CDR-RFS which is a mode for recording in packets, CDR-UDF which is the industry standard data recording mode, and CD-Text, devised by Philips for adding text to CD audio sequences (each heading is shown clearly on the unit while the CD audio is being played). The CD-Text format is being used by numerous software packages and seems to be becoming a standard.

Which standards and which CDs for your recording?

After reading about all these standards, modes and methods, your head will be spinning! No good going on about it, after

■■■ ■ ■ ■ ■ ■

all, there are only twelve hours a day for learning how to write disks! So now let's answer this vital question: what do you want to do with your CD writer?

■ Quick conclusion

Although we will come back to this in detail in Chapter 7, it will not be a waste of time to begin clearing the decks now. In short:

- the only truly universal readable organisation standard is ISO9660 (the Joliet is nevertheless today's standard, readable on all PCs equipped with Windows NT, 95 and 98);
- if it's written on a mono-session disk;
- being sure that the mono-session disk is in Mode 1.

Which leads us to advise you that these choices create a standard CD, but do not necessarily exploit all available possibilities. We can therefore do a lot better...

3
Technical characteristics of recording media

How does a recorder work?

Technologies, advantages and inconveniences

The technology of recorders, as described in Part II of the *Orange Book*, is scrupulously followed by all the machines on the market. It consists of the inscription of data by a photographic method on a photo-sensitive material. The reader will certainly understand that the precision of the laser and the density of inscribed data (nearly 600 tracks per millimetre) brings with it a host of constraints. And that these are the same constraints – poorly understood – that are the most frequent source of recording errors. It's therefore useful to understand how that works 'inside'! Do not neglect this 'technical education' aspect of the internal workings of your media. It will be valuable in resolving problems you'll meet. Let's begin with the most elementary process: that of the inscription of data.

■ How does a recorder work?

In Chapter 2 we have seen that the recording layer on CD-R media is composed of cyanine or phthalocyanine. You may know that these two compounds have photo-sensitive attributes. Their working principle is very close to that of a photographic film.

The process of data inscription is as follows: when the laser illuminates a point on the recording layer, the point of impact becomes opaque as a result of a chemical reaction. The process is laser-sharp and irreversible.

The architecture for a CD writer is therefore relatively simple. It's developed practically on the same principle as a CD-ROM player, that is, a turntable supporting a laser light emitter (although using a different wavelength from the player), the emitter being displaced laterally while the disk turns. By this procedure each recess of the CD-R can be swept by the laser, and therefore burnt.

Burning, excessive terminology?

We speak of recording media and of CD-R burning. If the process is photographic, is there a confusion and excess of terminology here? Probably: you could talk of printing or of developing, terms established in the photography field and hence better suited.

For uniformity however, we will use the expression CD burning unanimously adopted by users.

As you may know, this architecture is precise almost to a micron: you need absolute precision to allow illumination of points at regular intervals anywhere on the disk. The essential thing here is to follow the exact trace of the physical track on the CD-R, to the obvious end of compatibility with all CD-ROM drives, showing the importance of an uninterrupted flow of information during a burn operation.

The recording speed is non-variable

Once the recording process is launched, the speed is fixed and non-variable. A recorder burns the data in Mode 15 (150 KB/s), 25 (300 KB/s) and perhaps 45 (600 KB/s). The laser beam which burns the data, once started, maintains the same frequency to assure the precision of what it writes almost to the micron. A laser the write-frequency of which fluctuated would be incapable of writing data with sufficient precision and would produce non-readable disks.

A similar architecture for a player and recorder then, but a difference in build: the data reception electronics. While a CD-ROM drive only sends data to the PC, the recorder, like a hard disk, operates in both directions. The recorder is therefore connected to the PC by a bidirectional interface, capable of establishing a true dialogue with the computer.

It's also equipped with a complete storage mechanism in order to ensure a permanent supply of data in sufficient quantity: it's essential to maintain the flow of data when it's needed. These are the buffers. Modern recorders are often fitted with 1 MB data buffers. Certain models are also equipped with hard disks, assuring them of total control of data for recording. To sum up, a recorder is therefore:

- a laser head mounted on a transport mechanism
- some buffers
- a bi-directional interface

The flow is essential

The recorder is a tried and tested mechanism. Its only requirement is to receive a sufficiently steady flow of data for burning. Almost all recording faults are connected directly or indirectly to the data flow. The software? Its configuration influences the flow. The hard disk? Likewise. The recorder? Equally.

For all these reasons, we will mention the notion of flow in all the chapters to come.

■ Technologies, advantages and inconveniences

In the light of this technical information, you'll understand that the two most important electronic modules in a recorder are its buffers and the interface which connects it to the PC. Poor administration of these two components result in 90% of recording errors. What might cause such bad management?

- a badly configured interface
- a set of poor quality drivers
- a misused buffer
- a connection of insufficient speed between the computer and recorder
- a recording speed that your PC cannot match

Which interface to choose

Let's then examine the two interface possibilities for a recorder: the SCSI and the EIDE. Each component of a PC is connected to another component by a connector of some sort. Similar to a road connecting two houses or two towns. Anyway, it's this analogy which has led to the name 'bus' being used for the interface that receives all types of PC expansion cards (video card, sound card).

For our recorder, which is a 'mass memory' device in the style of a hard disk or a CD-ROM drive, it's the interface of that family of peripherals that will consequently be used.

 Mass memory

Mass memory means any device for data storage, re-writable or not. The expression is normally used for magnetic or optical devices, as opposed to 'electrical' memory such as the RAM or the ROM of a PC. A hard disk is a mass memory device, just like a CD-ROM drive or a backup tape cartridge.

The interface categories for mass memory devices are not numerous, and very well standardised. They are of two kinds: the IDE (evolved to EIDE), which equips almost all commercial PCs, and serves equally well for connecting hard disks as for CD-ROM internal drives, and the SCSI (evolved to Fast SCSI or SCSI 2).

This family of interfaces is very high-tech (and therefore pricey!). They are fitted as standard only on a few high-end PCs. They can receive from internal disks, but also, by a set of cables (connecting peripherals to each other in a chain), from external devices. Almost all the external archive devices (Seagate tape storage, Jazz disk recorder), are connected to the PC by a SCSI card.

We mention, if only anecdotally, the parallel interface, utilised for printers. Its set of electronic components allows it to send and receive data. It had therefore often been used to connect peripheral storage devices, even CD-ROM players. Some brave manufacturers have begun to propose connecting recorders to the parallel port: every man for himself!

Sophisticated interfaces such as the SCSI and the IDE already pose enough problems without wishing to add to them by using a primeval interface such as the parallel port!

The return of yesterday's problems

We think it's important here to recall a problem of years gone by, that has become an enduring legend: with the early printers, in fact, the marriage of the IDE and SCSI interfaces posed several problems. Problems essentially due to the fact that all recorders are driven with interfaces which simulate SCSI commands (the famous ASPI drivers) and that these drivers control IDE peripherals very badly. Today, no problem! All recorders, whether IDE or SCSI, are correctly managed as long as you are furnished with good ASPI drivers. These have in fact been constantly updated over recent months, and the mixing of SCSI hard disks with IDE recorders, or the other way round, does not pose problems any more.

The SCSI recorder

Let's consider the SCSI, closely tied to the story of CD-Rs. The first recorders were all intended for connection via SCSI interfaces: a legitimate choice, these offered all the features necessary for a recorder:

- good and constant data flow rate (at least 1 MB per second, while IDE cards of the period were much less reliable);
- 'Plug. and Play' interface: it's only necessary to install the device in the peripheral chain for it to be recognised.

Figure 3.1 Unlike internal IDE CD-ROM burners, SCSI burners are usually supplied as external drives.

Another advantage, the early players were bulky, and hence external devices. Only a SCSI card permitted the optimum connection of external devices. Reliability, efficiency, speed, all these advantages have a price: the cost of buying the card before the SCSI devices could be connected! Because the greater part of PCs were equipped as standard with an IDE interface (EIDE today), less quick and less pliable, a separate SCSI card purchase was needed.

The IDE recorder

Certain manufacturers have therefore tried to come up with recorders capable of exploiting the inbuilt and therefore free IDE interface. This is the case with Mitsumi, for example, or even with Philips, whose IDE models can be installed in PCs exactly like CD-ROM players or diskette drives. The recorder is connected to the EIDE interface by a ribbon cable connected directly to a free socket, or again by connecting to the second EIDE connector of an already existing ribbon cable. Please note, this type of recorder, which is also a player (and looks like it), cannot be considered as a satisfactory CD-ROM player: it's much too slow (the performance of the more recent models are of the order of those of a 4× average player), even if it's supposed to reach the speed of an 8×, or even a 16×, when reading. This slowness is due to the weight of the read heads which degrade the track by track access times.

On the other hand, as a recorder, as a copying tool (to make a copy of a disk) or as an audio CD copier (via the extract function to which we will return and which is present on all current IDE recorders), its performance is excellent.

But the advantages of IDE recorders are not only in their performance: their strong point, is that they use the existing interface, and that they are very compact since installed directly into the PC. They are, in general, controlled by an Atapi driver, relatively simple to install. We will come back to drivers in the next chapter.

The recording speed

And the speed? A recorder, that writes quickly? Let's say that the speed of recorders is described according to the same principles as those of CD-ROM players (see above). As for players, the speeds are multiples of the original *Red Book* speed: the 1×, say 150 KB/s. It's this unique speed which was adopted for the first recorders. But the 1× mode takes 72 minutes to record a CD of 650 MB: a little slow. Then came 2× recorders, which performed the same task in 36 minutes.

These two speeds, 15 and 25, are the only ones defined in the *Orange Book*, Part II. Higher recording speeds are not foreseen by the CD-R standard. This has not prevented certain manufacturers from going on to higher speeds.

Thus, the new Yamaha recorders are capable of creating CD-Rs in 65 or 85 mode, which permits a 650 MB CD to be recorded in 9 minutes! We have no doubt that some users will be seduced by the time saving that such high-speed CD-R creation can offer.

Standard speeds will evolve considerably in the coming months but it's necessary to draw attention to the risks connected to the configuration.

We are in fact obliged to return here to the problem of flow: if nearly all PCs, beginning with the 486 DX4/100s, are capable of burning a CD in 1× mode, the same does not apply for the 2× and yet less for the 4×. Imagine that if 150 KB/s is enough to record a CD in 1× mode, then 600 KB are needed in 4× mode. With a flow rate of 599.9 KB, the recorder grinds to a halt! So, even if numerous PCs are capable of reaching or even surpassing this hi-tech flowrate, rare are those which manage to maintain it for 18 minutes at a stretch.

Let's say that, for now, and up to the Pentium 166, it's preferable to limit recording to 25 mode in order to reduce to the minimum the risk of faulty CD-R recordings. For the recent servers (Pentium II at 300 Mhz and above, K6-3D), compatibles (equipped with high-speed hard disks) and correctly configured, it's quite possible to record at high speed. We know now:

- the standards proposed by the *Orange Book* are limited to a 2× recording speed only
- higher recording speeds above 4× are not standard but imposed by the market
- the times necessary for recording a CD are as follows:
  - a 650 MB CD is recorded in 72 minutes in 1× mode;
  - a 650 MB CD is recorded in 36 minutes in 2× mode;
  - a 650 MB CD is recorded in 18 minutes in 4× mode;
  - a 650 MB CD is recorded in 9 minutes in 8× mode.

These speeds are invariable, but be careful: certain ancillary operations can considerably increase the time taken to record a CD-R. The writing of the 'table of contents', for example, can take several minutes. Also, don't forget to take into account the time taken by the software to construct the file it's going to record. We will come back to this.

Internal or external player?

Several details remain to be examined as far as recorders are concerned. A question, for example, which most users always ask concerns the difference between internal and external players. The answer is simple: no preference. On the other hand there are some facts:

- All EIDE recorders are internal.
- Those functioning on SCSI cards are more often external, occasionally internal.
- Only the EIDE interface, strongly recommended for the price savings it offers, necessitates an internal player. The rest is up to you. Whether or not too use desk space is for you to decide.

Can you think of a recorder as a player?

Another important point: the use of the recorder as a player. Since nearly all can be used to read CD-ROMs, it's therefore tempting to want to concentrate both functions into a single drive. You should realise however that this feature is not without problems: the electronic and mechanical components of recorders are much heavier than those of players. The result, a very appreciable fall in performance, and often a speed limited in reality to 4× mode (sometimes 6×), even if the wrapper claims a higher performance. The conclusion in axiomatic format: always accompany the recorder with a CD-ROM player. For less than £100, you can nowadays buy an 8× player which will give you complete satisfaction, and as we will see in the rubric on software packs, will even provide you with a series of additional functionalities.

Some materials

It is a myth to think that materials don't matter much. A disk *x* can be recorded on recorder *y*, but not on another recorder of brand *z*! This is the case, of some karaoke CD+G disks which are replayable only on a limited number of players. Others meet with 'firmware' problems, the built-in software of the recorder, which may be incompatible with certain functions of recorder software packages. In a book like this it's impossible to test all the recorders on the market. Nevertheless here are a few drives recommended for their quality. Some, you'll see, have some bugs: just be aware of these. The absence of an audio outlet on a recorder, for example, is perhaps compensated for by a good quality CD-ROM player that takes care of it:

- Yamaha CDR100/102/200/400. The only unit compatible with everything, including CD+Gs, with absolutely up to date firmware. Expensive, but of very high standard.

- Ricoh 1420 C. A very good unit, but careful of those models equipped with Firmware version 1.6, which is not capable of audio extraction.

- Sony 920S/924S. A reliable unit, compatible with everything, quick and friendly.

- Philips CDD2000 (known under the brand name HP4020i). The older versions (end of 1995, if you buy second hand) have some firmware problems, and cause numerous bugs.

- Philips CDD2600 (known under the brand name HP6020i). This is a reliable unit, but has problems extracting audio. It's impossible to update the firmware, which leads you to believe that the audio defect might be incurable.

- Mitsumi CR2600 TE. A remarkable IDE unit. Capable of everything, speedy. No particular compatibility problems.

It seems appropriate to add some technical details for the players mentioned above, tested by the author for different publications. The JVC, amongst others, which could not be tested, seems to be recommended by numerous authors, and is above all one of the rare units capable of recording in 4× mode.

HP SureStore CD writer 6020es 6×/2× CD-R (£300)

Type of recorder	CD-R
Internal or external	External
Recording capacity	650 MB
Average access time	400 ms
Data reading speed	6×
Data writing speed	2×
Interface	SCSI
Family	SCSI-2
Interface included	No

Mitsumi CR2600 TE (£300)

Type of recorder	CD-R
Internal or external	Internal
Recording capacity	650 MB
Average access time	350 ms
Data reading speed	6×
Data writing speed	2×
Interface	IDE
Family	EIDE
Interface included	Not applicable/ ATAPI driver supplied

JVC Personal Archiver Plus 4×/4× CD-R £650
(or £700 for external version)

Type of recorder	CD-R
Internal or external	Internal
Recording capacity	650 MB
Average access time	390 ms
Data reading speed	4×
Data writing speed	4×
Interface	SCSI
Family	SCSI-2
Interface included	SCSI-2

What to select

A list of hardware, that's fine; to know how to choose
according to your needs, that's better still! Here are some
practical hints to follow.

According to your equipment

Let's start with the interfaces:

- If your PC is equipped with a EIDE interface:
  - If you wish to equip at the lowest price, buy a Mitsumi
    EIDE recorder.
  - If you want the best possible performance, buy a
    recorder with SCSI card (Philips CDD for example).
- If your PC is fitted with a SCSI interface:
  - Purchase a SCSI recorder, without interface card.

Furthermore, you should take the performance of your
machine into account. Thus:

- If your PC is better than a Pentium 166:
  - You can choose a CD-R 4× speed or above but you
    should probably limit the recording speed to 2× mode.

- If your PC is lower than the Pentium 166:
  - For preference choose a high-performance CD-R, and use it in 1× mode, the only mode capable of producing CD-Rs without risk of frequent error.
- If your PC is a Pentium II 300 or better:
  - You can, if you have the means, buy a 8× speed recorder in conjunction with a good quality SCSI-2 interface card.

How many CDs per year, per week... day... hour?

One other question that some users might have to ask themselves is that of needs in terms of quantity produced. The choice here depends on the work habits of the user. Some examples:

- The CD-R is used once or twice a week to make hard disk copies, archives, prototype multimedia CDs.
- The CD-R is used at least once a day for the above same purposes, because there is more than one user.
- The CD-R is used up to ten times a day, for example in the provision of a service.
- The CD-R is used at spaced intervals, but to make sizeable runs of CDs, for example, of technical documentation.

As you may note, the utilisation profiles are innumerable. It's difficult to recommend a particular configuration for each case. Here, you enter into the world of production planning. A few instances however:

- As far as long runs are concerned, you should evaluate the economic advantage of the CD-R. Be aware, for example, that above 1,000 CDs, some disk duplicators offer better prices. They include the master, the run, with screen printing, sometimes for less than £600. Compare this with the cost of the equipment, of the CD-R disks, of the operator...

Not forgetting that 1,000 industrially copied CDs are less expensive, in this case, than 500 CD-Rs!

- In the case of small consecutive runs (from 100 to 200 CDs), you should calculate the time at your disposal, and choose suitable hardware. With a 4× recorder, for example, you are theoretically in a position to produce a CD-R every 18 minutes. In actual practice, including handling, software management time, and some misfires, you'll probably not do better than 2 CDs per hour, say about 15 per working day, so you would need a battery of recorders, or to extend the operation over several days.

- If you are providing a service, or recording for internal needs, calculate the needs of your clients or of your services and then choose from the 1×, 2×, 4× speed recorders. Some clients are ready to pay extra for a CD recorded in less than 30 minutes, so think about it...

- Remember also that a recorder used for copying or mastering must be available to those who need it. This implies that it is installed on a machine reserved for it, rather than on the machine of a colleague who will become annoyed at being disturbed at regular intervals!

- If you are a user 'at leisure', let's say, then time may be less important. Therefore do what you want to suit your pocket! But remember to choose a machine that supports all the software functions: the leisure-user, no matter what else, is a veritable dabbler in everything!

Remember also that not all CD-Rs are necessarily full, and that it only takes a few minutes to record 10 MB of data on a CD-R in 2× mode. A production run on this model might be feasible. In conclusion:

- The CD-R is always suited to recording one-offs.
- The CD-R is sometimes suitable for consecutive runs of less than 300 disks. It will require careful evaluation of production time and a good work plan.

Special recording installations

For medium runs, from 100 to 500 off, special so-called 'Jukebox' installations are on the market and comprise several CD-Rs in a battery, recording simultaneously. These are expensive installations (several thousand pounds), but can be very useful.

4 Installation of the PC CD recorder

To install an EIDE recorder
To install a SCSI recorder
Extra peripherals

The recorder has been purchased? The beast in its box waits imperiously on your desk, and you burn with impatience to duplicate CDs by the hundred? Fine, but before we can play with it there are some preliminaries to be taken care of. Such is life! So, shall we begin?

If you are struggling, have it installed!

Allergic to spanners? Revolted by screwdrivers? Waste neither time nor energy on the installation: ask your supplier to do it (even if it does cost a few pounds). He will take care of everything and you can go directly to Chapter 6, ready to record, copy and duplicate!

■ To install an EIDE recorder

An internal mounting is required for the recorder. So make a start by opening your computer and finding a free expansion bay: one of the 'metal drawers' designated to hold a 5¼" drive unit. They are located at the top of the front face side of tower system units, and on the left or right of the front face of desk-top units. Choose a bay, remove the plastic mask, then insert the recorder and use the fixing screws.

The installation of an IDE recorder should not pose too much of a problem if you have already installed an IDE CD-ROM player or hard disk in your machine. In short, there are three steps to take: select the connecting ribbon cable, connect up to this cable, then set the jumpers on the recorder to 'master' or 'slave' mode. Don't forget the power!

Master and slave principle

IDE connectors on recent PCs are usually two in number. To each connector, two peripherals can be allotted. The premier peripheral being in 'master' mode, the second in 'slave' mode. Note that some hard disks can be configured in 'master only' mode, 'master with slave' mode, or 'slave only mode'. If you link the recorder to the disk as a slave, you should check its configuration and change its jumper settings to 'master with slave'.

Let's begin then by evaluating our installation options so as to determine the settings for the recorder jumpers. The PC is open? Let's have a look! Several solutions are possible:

- The PC is equipped with a hard disk and a CD-ROM player in slave or master mode on the second cable. The recorder will use this second cable connector to be connected in master mode to the IDE CD player of the PC.

- The PC is equipped with two hard disks on the first interface, and a CD-ROM player on the second. The recorder will be master of the CD-ROM player and installed on the connector of the free remaining cable.

PC too old!

If you try to install a IDE recorder on a PC that is too old (certain 486 DX4/100, even the first Pentiums), it's possible that the installed IDE interface will accept only two peripherals. If, unfortunately for you, the PC in question is already equipped with a hard disk and a CD-ROM player, there is no place left for the recorder. In this particular case, you should favour the SCSI recorder solution, and install a SCSI card in your PC.

To help you, here are some examples of switch configurations on an IDE Mitsumi CR-2600 TE (1). You can make use of these tables according to the configuration which corresponds to your PC. Once the configuration is found, you configure the corresponding switch on the recorder. It's labelled simply 'master' or 'slave' mode, and located on the rear of the apparatus.

The Mitsumi recorder

The Mitsumi EIDE recorders resemble CD players in many ways. They are similar in appearance and are installed in a 5¹/₄" bay. They also use the 'master and slave' modes.

Figure 4.1 Yhe Mitsumi recorder.

Table 4.1 Hard disk and CD-ROM already installed on two IDE connections.

IDE Connection	Master	Slave
Primary	Hard Disk	
Secondary	CD-ROM	Recorder

Table 4.2 Two hard disks and one CD-ROM already installed on two IDE connections.

IDE Connection	Master	Slave
Primary	Hard Disk	DD (2)
Secondary	Recorder	CD-ROM

(1) These tables apply to all IDE recorders on the market. Consult your IDE recorder documentation to find the location of the switches.

(2) Check that the hard disk is not configured in 'master only' mode. Read the above.

Everything is installed? Configured? All that remains is to link the connector on the ribbon cable to the connector on the CD-R (using the connector guide), then to connect one of the supplied power cables to the recorder. That's all. Go directly to the 'attached peripherals' stage to refine your configuration.

■ To install a SCSI recorder

Existing interface or not

If your PC is already equipped with a correctly configured SCSI card, you are spared the (annoying) operations below. Go directly to the next stage! If, on the other hand, your recorder has been delivered with an interface, you have to install and configure it.

First stage, which moreover raises more of the classic installation of a peripheral than of a recorder: check for conflicts. Your card must have an IRQ address, DMA, an area of memory, and input/output ports. The base configuration is normally 130 for the inputs and outputs, D000 for the memory area, 9 for the IRQ, and 7 for the DMA. Take careful note of these parameters which will probably be requested during the software configuration:

■ If your card is Plug and Play (type 1542 C from Adaptec), you don't have any switches/jumpers to set. For now, install the card in a free slot, that's all!

■ If your card is provided with switches, consult the documentation to set them according to the configuration we have just given.

Internal or external

The card is installed, now to install the recorder. There are two possibilities: it's external or internal. In either case, SCSI peripherals must be allotted an ID number. On external peripherals, there is a wheel for setting a number. On internal peripherals there is a set of jumpers. The number 5 has less chance of being reserved. Never use numbers 0 or 1 (often used by hard disks), or number 7 (allotted to the card). If you have just installed the card, no problem, number 4 must be free. If the card was already present in the PC, check what SCSI peripherals are already installed (scanner, CD-ROM, hard disks, backups) and avoid the same numbers. Select a free number.

- If the player is internal, connect it to one of the free connectors on the SCSI cable. If no connector is available, buy a SCSI auxiliary cable. That's all!

- If the player is external, check that the cables are type SCSI 2 (small connector similar in size to the parallel interface), or SCSI (large connectors). Connect one of the two plugs of the recorder to the output socket of the SCSI card, then put a terminator over the second free plug.

- That's all for the moment. With a little luck, all will be well, and you'll not have to configure any software. We will see in the next chapter!

■ Extra peripherals

You'll probably need other peripherals for recording your CD-ROMs. A sound card, if you want to transform musical data into audio sequences, and a CD player to make copies 'track by track' or to extract sounds.

The sound card

It must be standard, and if you want to use it for recording audio tracks, for example retrieved from a vinyl record, make sure that the card is of very good quality, capable, in fact, of opening, reading and producing 44 kHz, 16-bit, stereo sound files. Only such cards will be of a standard high enough to exploit the capacity of your future CD-Rs.

The CD-ROM player

The CD-ROM player can be used in two ways:

- **Copying from CD to CD-R.** You insert a disk into the player for it to be copied in real time by the recorder.

- **Extracting audio information.** Sound sequences are extracted directly in CD audio (*Red Book*) format, and not PC .wav format, and you then record them on a CD for replay on your audio CD player.

For both these activities, check that the speed of your CD player is sufficient. It's no good trying to copy from disk to disk on a 4× recorder if your player is not up to it! The flow is critical. Let's say that if you apply the following rules, you should be able to make good-quality copies from disk to disk:

- recorder in mode 1×, 2× CD-ROM player acceptable, 4× is ideal;

- recorder in mode 2×, CD-ROM player 8× at least, 16× is ideal;

- recorder in mode 4×, CD-ROM player 8× at least, higher is better still;

- recorder in mode 8×, CD-ROM player 16× high performance.

You must also understand that to extract tracks from an audio disk, and record them as such, your player must have the function 'Extraction Digital Audio'. This is not the case for all players sold over the years, although nearly all recent players are so equipped.

A video acquisition card

You may be wanting to create video-CDs compatible with the specifications of the *White Book* and hence readable on Philips video-CD players. We will not dwell on this technique which requires a large set up. However, be advised that it's technically possible to transform a video disk, or a camcorder or video-recorder cassette into a video-CD. The operation is possible if you are the owner of a video card capable of transferring 2 MB/s of video data, in full PAL format resolution, with a low level of compression. Suffice it to say that you'll need a K6-2 running at 300 Mhz, at least, equipped at the minimum with a DC 20 Miro card, a DC 30 being better!

5 Configuration, drivers and the Internet

■■

Hardware correctly installed? It's time to configure it! It's imperative to do this before installing the recording software. In fact, the recording software accesses recorders via a standardised software interface: the driver. If this interface is missing, the software is incapable of recognizing the recorder or of using it.

Happily, it's becoming more and more frequent, with Windows 98, for hardware to be detected and the drivers to be installed automatically. That was already the case with Windows 95, but with a little less success.

With Windows 98 the procedure is simple:

- Switch off the machine.
- Connect the recorder to the system unit and switch the recorder on.
- Switch on the computer.
- Windows 98 will detect the new hardware and install a driver for it.

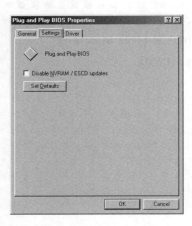

Figure 5.1 The 'Plug and Play' of Windows 95 and 98.

With Windows 3.1, it's much more complicated. You must install the drivers manually. With MS-DOS, it's a real grind, and frankly old hat. This book will therefore proceed on the basis that your PC is equipped with Windows 95 at worst, but better still Windows 98, for the installation of the recorder.

Your PC is probably plug and play. To reassure yourself, select the system option on the control panel and check that the 'plug and play' driver has really been installed. By double-clicking on the icon, you'll display the window shown in Figure 5.1. If all is working as it should, your card will be automatically detected at start-up, and a 'detection' window will be displayed.

■ Recorder drivers and their importance

Drivers for SCSI recorders

Logically, if the SCSI card was already installed in the system, it's probable that your recorder will be recognised the moment it's connected to the chain. If this is not the case, you have a configuration problem and should review certain parameters.

If you are installing a SCSI card at the same time, the automatic recognition procedure by Windows 95 or 98 will cut in, especially if the card is of PCI type. The card will then be installed and the assembly will be ready to work.

You'll find excellent information on installation problems for SCSI cards at the following addresses:

> http://www.adaptec.com/support/faqs/win95.html
> http://www.adaptec.com/support/manuals/
> installation.html

Adaptec is the main manufacturer of PC SCSI cards. You'll probably find all the drivers you need on their Internet site.

Figure 5.2 Adaptec on the Internet.

SCSI configuration hints and tips

For the majority of Adaptec SCSI cards, as well as for those
of other brands, make sure that the configuration corresponds to the following points:

- Deactivate the 'Synchronous negotiation' option.
- Set the transfer speed as low as possible (from 1 to 5
  MB/s). On the Adaptec 154X cards, deactivate the Fast
  SCSI option.
- Validate the option 'Enable disconnection'.

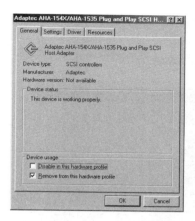

Figure 5.3 Windows 95 and Adaptec cards.

- It can sometimes be mandatory to leave a SCSI recorder uniquely on a card.
- With Windows 95, deactivate the BIOS support option, and the interrupt 13 support option.
- With Windows 98, everything should be automatic (that's the theory, at least!)

 With Windows 95 and 98, SCSI products are supported automatically. The system driver takes care of everything: you will therefore not require the BIOS on your card, which should be deactivated.

Drivers for IDE recorders

The IDE recorder, after installation, is automatically recognised by the hardware, but needs a driver to be recognised by the operating system. It's almost certain that this driver will be installed by Windows 95 and Windows 98, from machine start-up. Otherwise, use the installation procedure on

Figure 5.4 Config.sys and the drivers.

diskette and execute the *Setup.exe* program which will perform the operation.

The procedure includes the addition to your *config.sys* file of an ATAPI driver line which supports the recorder. You may have to change this driver, if new versions appear on the market. The IDE recorders driver is installed in the *config.sys* file, exactly as for a CD-ROM player.

Using the Internet

In every case, whether for a SCSI or an IDE card, to avoid errors and malfunctions, it is of fundamental importance that the drivers should be kept absolutely up to date. Check the version number of the driver in the configuration panel of Windows 95 or 98, system options, and make sure that no more recent drivers are available via the manufacturers' Internet sites.

If you use an Adaptec SCSI card, made sure that this has the most recently updated drivers. They are available at the following addresses:

ftp://ftp.adaptec.com/pub/BBS/win95/win95mpd.exe
ftp://ftp.adaptec.com/pub/BBS/win95/aspi32.exe

For ASPI (SCSI) or ATAPI (IDE) standard Windows 95 drivers, look up the section on drivers in the site:

http://www.microsoft.com

Also use the sites of PC manufacturers, and of your recorder manufacturer. Here are some of their Web sites:

http://www.plasmon.com
http://www.hp.com
http://www.mitsumi.com
http://www.yamahayst.com
http://www.sony.com

MSCDEX

If you are equipped with old CD players, running under Windows 95, or even Windows 98, you should also check that the version of MSCDEX, the CD-ROM driver for your PC, is absolutely up to date. In fact, versions numbered below 2.23 seem to instigate problems, causing amongst others warnings of 'incorrect file names', or worse, 'files not found' although the CDs are correctly recorded. This driver has no bearing on recording, but it can set problems for you at replay time and lead you astray by mistake. So check that it's really up to date.

Windows 98 detects all CD players automatically, Windows 95, linked to a modern IDE player, likewise. No problems with MSCDEX then, in either case.

Firmware

Firmware is the wired-in 'brain' of a recorder, a little like the BIOS of a PC. If you buy a new recorder, you need not concern yourself with this control program. On the other hand, if your recorder is second hand, it's likely that some updates may have been made. Careful, some recorders cannot be updated (they are best avoided anyway).

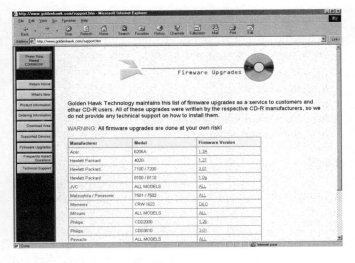

Figure 5.5 The firmware is important.

How to find out your firmware version? With a little luck, at start-up your SCSI card or IDE will display a table of connected peripherals, and will show the firmware version number in one column.

On a Windows 95 or 98 PC, you only need to select the recorder icon in the configuration panel, System option, then to click on the Drivers or Resources tab. The number should be listed opposite the Firmware revision field.

Then, on the recorder manufacturer's Internet site, check the date of the latest firmware revision. If needs be, when there is a new version, download it then run the program. Everything should run automatically.

 In numerous cases it will be possible to update the recorder by using new 'firmware'. Check on this important option before buying your hardware.

■ Installing the software

Our hardware is correctly installed. It's therefore time to go on to installing the software. In most cases, it will be Easy CD from Adaptec, or Nero from Ahead, or WinOnCD from CeQuadrat, which will have been supplied. No problem. Start the installation program, and everything should run automatically.

If you have bought a recorder without software, check before buying any to make sure it's compatible with your hardware. Lists on this matter are available from the publishers.

That's it, the next chapter deals with recording practice!

6 What the software can do!

■ ■

Be wise...

A thousand and one ways of copying

Recording without... copying!

Everything is ready: a pile of original media await your work plan. Of all types: you wish to transfer your video-cassettes on to video CDs, to create CD-ROM backup copies, to compile audio collections for the CD player in your car. You want to do everything, quickly, and well! That's understandable. So much so that we are going to explain the 'how' to you! But before going ahead, a word of caution... a legal word at that!

■ Be wise...

Because if we are going to give you the information on how to copy all existing forms of CD, you should be aware that there are also rules of good conduct. Take care, there is nothing illegal in anything that is written here, and no secrets will be betrayed. But there are laws, and behind these laws there are authors. Here we go then on the rights of authors! Rather than set them out, I prefer to try to make you understand their usefulness:

■ I would not appreciate you photocopying this book to make a present of it to hundreds of recording software users. I have worked too hard in writing it: I have earned my author's rights!

■ A CD-ROM author who has invested much of his time so that you can share in his passion, merits a just reward. To copy his CD to give it away is not an honest way to behave.

That, you tell me, is someone else's problem... Let's see!

■ You are an engineer and the industrial products which assure your salary are plagiarised in Asia, your employer's business is likely to fail and you are redundant: hard luck.

■ You study information technology at university and you copy some software that they use: don't complain later if the publishers do not hire young graduates: 30% of their profits are sometimes lost through piracy... You know full well that your job would have been financed by that 30%.

Copy honestly, but do not steal! Make a compilation of your audio CDs for your car or for convenience, it's not forbidden provided you bought the originals. Make a single copy of any CD to preserve the original, that is OK. Distribute, reproduce in quantity, commercialise... strictly forbidden and the punishment is severe: think about it.

Enough or not, here endeth the morality lesson... back to the grind!

■ A thousand and one ways of copying

Anything can be copied with a recorder and CD player provided the hardware and software are up to the job. In practice, there are two main types of copy:

- **The logical copy.** This consists in transferring the content of a CD to a hard disk, then reorganising and re-recording it.
- **The physical copy.** This is not concerned with the file structures or data standards of the disk contents. The CD is copied, track by track, sector by sector, bit by bit.

Physical copy against logical copy

For the same disk, it's sometimes possible to apply either of the copy methods. Take the case of an audio CD disk. If we want to copy it as it stands, we reproduce it track for track to obtain a perfect clone. That is a physical copy.

On the other hand, if we seek to retrieve only a few sound tracks, or to reorganise them, we will extract each track one by one, reorganise them with special software, and re-record the whole on a new CD-R. That's a logical copy.

Which software for which type of copy?

As regards the logical copy, there are classic software programs for making CDs such as Easy CD Creator or Easy CD Pro which will do the job. Simply transfer the data on to hard disk, reorganise it with the software, then re-record it to make a copy.

For the physical copy, the most polished software currently available is the CDRWIN utility, available in trial version limited to recording Mode 1× on the Internet site of its publisher, **www.goldenhawk.com**. It does everything: you insert a CD, it's analysed, the type of disk (Audio, CD-ROM Mode 1, Mode 2, mixed mode, and CD+G) is determined and a copy is made. It goes without saying that CDRWIN can recopy almost anything: CD-Is or video-CDs, for example. All disks written in Mode 2 and multisessions are also perfectly catered for. We will return to this. The program costs around £50.

Return to Snapshot

For the record, we said in our previous edition that the software program Snapshot, from the same publisher as CDRWIN, was the ideal copy utility. This DOS utility is obsolete from now on because it's much too complicated. Be aware also that CDRWIN works much better, much more efficiently and more quickly. So...

Some utilities, such as 'snapshot', were the first accessory programs on the market for making 'physical disk copies': they are useful when duplicating 'file by file' is impossible. They have nevertheless been replaced by more polished Windows utilities such as CDRWIN or Gear.

Let's examine all the possibilities for duplicating a CD case by case.

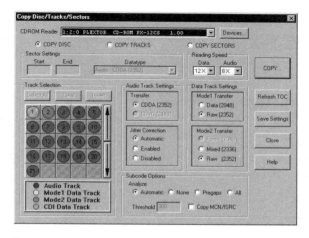

Figure 6.1 A physical copy utility.

Copying an audio CD

There are several ways to copy an audio disk:

- Digitising the sound with a sound card and storing it in Wav format on the hard disk (see Figure 6.2). Then reconverting it with CD manufacturing software to audio CD format, and re-writing it to a CD-R. This is a bad solution, which takes a lot of time, and results in a loss of sound quality. It's reserved for the copying of audio tapes, cassettes, or vinyl records, on to CD.

- The best solution is the 100% digital: extracting some tracks directly from the audio CD, and then digitally re-recording these tracks.

It's this last solution that we will focus on. Software programs reduced to their most simple form, such as 'Spin Doctor' from Adaptec, have moreover concentrated on this

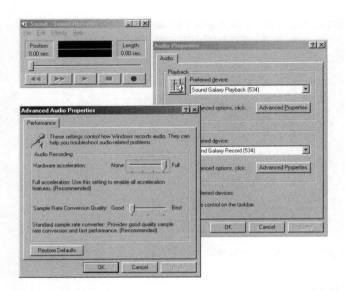

Figure 6.2 With Sound Recorder anything is possible!.

single function. But beware, not all CD players extract audio tracks at the same speed. Thus, the NEC6Xi player is capable of extracting only at 1× speed, while the Plextor 6plex functions perfectly in extraction mode 6×. You have grasped it, with a 6× extractor, it will be possible to record also at 2× speed, while with a 2× or 1× extractor, you'll be obliged to store data temporarily on the hard disk.

In every case, you can store sound data on the disk, and organise the data as you see fit before re-recording, for example with Easy CD or CD Creator. That is the main advantage of copying audio CDs by the extraction method: it allows the creation of 'compilations' to order.

Windows Sound Recorder accessory program can be used to copy from any sound source except the one contained on an audio CD. There may be a loss in quality, notably due to the poor quality of the source.

 You should be aware that the extraction of audio data is an exact replica of audio CDs copied, as seen by your CD-ROM player! Some, in fact, do not read the whole sum of the audio bits and therefore only partly restore the original quality. That said, the differences are rarely audible.

Copying a CD-ROM

Copying a CD-ROM disk is the easiest since it's a question of retrieving some files and transferring them. It's a question therefore, whether to make a disk-to-disk copy using the recording software functions, or to copy the contents of the CD-ROM on to a hard disk, then to rewrite it. In this case, copying is very simple: Windows Explorer or the Macintosh finder utility will suffice! Be careful when copying by the 'ISO image' method exploited for example by the CD Copy module of WinOnCD or even CDRWIN. It allows the retrieval of the contents of a disk in image form (a file) stored on the hard disk without paying attention to the organisation or the content. You should realise that an ISO image takes up lots of space on disk, and that it obliges you to re-record on a CD-R of a capacity greater or equal to the original. Sometimes this poses problems, notably with 'overburning' protection that we are going to study now.

Overburning...

In fact, you'll often have problems when copying, caused by the industrial use of a particular recording mode – over-burning (which I discuss in detail in another book, *A CD recording starter*). This method allows writing to disk a little more than the 74 minutes theoretically available, by an ingenious process and the help of special machines. The result? All the software programs used for copying are thrown into disarray by the ISO image which they cannot extract (too extensive) and even less record (media too short!). At the time of writing, only Nero version 4 software, in combination with CD-Rs designed for overburning (they are beginning to appear in the shops), is capable of duplicating this type of product.

The majority of CD-ROMs on the market are not protected against copying, because they favour a system of recording using serial numbers. This is the same with practically all CD-ROM systems, shareware or commercial. Numerous CD games, on the other hand, are protected by various methods (see the end of this chapter for more details).

Copying console CDs from Sony Playstation, Sega Saturn, 3DO

Here, physical copying applies lead by CDRWIN. In fact, under certain conditions it allows re-copying of console-CDs. In some cases, when 'protections while writing' or 'error simulations' are activated, it is possible that copying might succeed, but that the disk could be unreadable.

In this case, the console CD is correctly copied, but the protection device is not written in, and the console refuses to read the disk. The console must be modified by adding to it a small processor called the 'Modchip', which allows such copies to be read. We do not have space to develop this subject. It's dealt with in detail in another book, *CD Recording* published by Macmillan, with numerous practical tips and a multitude of Internet addresses.

How to copy and make video CDs

If you hope to create video CDs corresponding to the *White Book* for video CDs, and that these CDs might be readable with a video CD player (or a CD-I), you must first of all be equipped with a bundle of software capable of creating the appropriate MPEG format. The creation of a video CD follows the following procedure:

- create the video file in MPEG format compatible with the *White Book*;

- write the CD-R using this file and following the *White Book* specifications.

The CD Creator software program was the first utility capable in theory of transforming AVI files retrieved by your graphics card into MPEG files. In doing this, Corel has taken certain liberties with the MPEG format, and the disks thus created run only rarely! Happily, other programs have come on the market, many more successful: WinOnCd for example, or again AV12MPG1 (available at the address **http://www.mnsi.net/~jschlic1/**) are excellent converters.

Once your video sequence is in the proper format, you can use the software packet 'Video CD Creator', delivered with Easy CD Creator to create a disk which is 100% compatible with video CD players. WinOnCd has the same mechanism for making video CDs compatible with Philips consoles.

And the copy?

To copy an existing disk, it's even easier (see Figure 6.3): the technique consists of the retrieval of the file structure contained on the video CD (ISO9660 compatible) by copying it to a hard disk, then rewriting to a CD-R using *White Book* formats either:

- Mode 2, Form 2;
- ISO9660 file structure.

A simple copying of files from disk to disk, such as we describe in Chapter 8, for files or CD-ROMs!

The video CD is recorded with ISO9660 file structure, and in standard mode. You can therefore read it on a PC without difficulty, and recopy it with the methods for duplicating CD-ROMs.

Figure 6.3 A video CD is readable on the PC!

How to copy a CD-I

To copy a CD-I, you follow a procedure identical to that used for video CDs. You only need to copy the contents of the CD-I to your hard disk, then to re-record the lot using CD-I specifications whether Mode 2, Form 2, or ISO9660 file structure.

How to copy karaoke CD+G disks

The CD+G standard is used by disks dedicated to karaoke machines. This standard allows the simultaneous screening of images or sub-titles during the performance of a song. Unfortunately, karaoke machines use a special logic.

Result: the disks can only be reproduced using selected recorders. These must in fact be equipped with a software program capable of reproducing the specific 'code' of CD+G disks. The following recorders are compatible:

- Creative CDR4210;
- Panasonic CW-7501;

- Plasmon CDR4240;
- Sony CDW-900 E;
- All Yamaha models.

Another point: to copy these disks, you must be able to read them! For these too, there are restrictions. Only Yamaha models CDR200 and CDR400 are capable of reading and writing CD+G disks.

Otherwise, the following recorders are themselves also capable of reading CD+G disks:

- Plextor 4Plex Plus, 8Plex, 12 Plex, Plextor 12/20Plex and Sony 76S (the last is not always compatible).

You have therefore several compatibility problems to resolve before concerning yourself with the logical part of this duplication. Because, to duplicate CD+G disks, specialised software is also needed: DAO.EXE under DOS or better still CDRWIN, capable not only of copying audio disks, CD-ROMs in modes 1 and 2, as well as CD+Gs. You can obtain these programs (in trial version), at the address: **http://www. goldenhawk.com/**

How to copy a Photo-CD

Kodak Photo-CDs exploit CD-ROM XA in Mode 2. You must therefore be equipped with a recorder which supports these modes in order to be able to copy these disks. But note! The Kodak recording format is patented, and therefore very widely protected. Moreover, to ensure that copying their disks will be difficult, Kodak invented a multi-session system which differs from CD-ROM standards. While in a CD-R or a CD-ROM, each session contains its own file structure, with Kodak Photo-CDs, the data relative to file organisation is organised so that information seems to be accumulated into a single volume. Physical-copy software is therefore necessary to reproduce this organisation. Here again, the track by

Figure 6.4 Kodak is protected!

track duplicator CDRWIN in its very latest version is the best adapted for freeing you from the reorganisational constraints of the file structure. You can also use Kodak software, which, unfortunately, only works with their own recorders. For more information contact:

http://www.kodak.com/digitalImaging/aboutPhotoCD/
aboutPCD.shtml

 Photo-CD and protection
Kodak Photo-CDs are well protected: only Kodak software utilities such as Multi Write allow their duplication and manipulation.

Notes on protection in force for CDs

Though they are easily reproducible in nearly all formats, CDs can sometimes be protected. It's difficult to find out the protection techniques in force. Developers are not very keen to reveal their techniques to the public (understandably)! Nevertheless, for those who hope to protect their works, here is an outline of some of the protection techniques in use.

In the first place, like in the good old days of diskette protection, it's by 'clever hacking' at the file structure that they most often try to protect CDs. The principle is simple: at a copy attempt, try to lead the operating system (DOS or Windows) into an error, without affecting simpler operations. You can read the media, but it's impossible to copy it with standard methods.

Doctoring the file structure

The most widespread of these techniques consists of an increase in the size of several files until these end up by taking up hundreds of megabytes. Hint: it's not the files themselves that are bulky! In fact, only the directory entry is modified, to make it appear that the files are much larger than they are! Thus, while the application handles files, everything functions correctly, but as soon as a copy attempt is made, the operating system does not understand further why the real length of the files is not what the disk structure is telling it. Result? Abort, Retry, or Cancel! This technique is generally circumvented by pirates by making a 'track by track' copy of the disk. In that case, the data and not the structure is copied, and the protection doesn't work any more.

Non-reproducible track and signature

Industrial CDs are able to handle a data zone beyond the 74 minutes, which is free in theory: remember 'overburning' mentioned earlier? What's more, this zone is actually readable by CD-ROM drives. The result is that what the computer can read, the recorder cannot copy, since its range is strictly limited to 74 minutes. This is quite an efficient method, since recorders and their software are usually not able to reproduce this zone: although the latest models, armed with appropriate software, are capable of it.

In the same spirit, the TTR company (**http://www.ttr.co.il**) confirms that it has developed a utility called 'DiskGuard'

Figure 6.5 Anti-pirate CDs are available!

(see Figure 6.5), which consists of a signature pressed into industrial CDs. There again, the CD players can read it, but cannot reproduce it. On its site, TTR presents a very hi-tech signature-based anti-copy utility. It comprises a signature, industrially recorded, but not reproducible by a recorder.

In both these scenarios, for the protection to be active, it's necessary that a software function, added to the application contained on the CD, reads this 'impossible to reproduce' data and verifies its validity. The action of this bit of code is simple: signature correct, the CD is original; signature incorrect or missing, the CD is a forgery. These protections are high-level since they oblige the pirate to copy the CD to disk in its entirety, then to use the PC or Mac system tools to identify the portion of verification code to deactivate it. In general, the more effective the protection, the shorter the verification program. It can work in some fifty bytes written in assembler, coded, for example, by the application of the XOR operator to each of the bytes composing the protection program.

Erroneous sectors

A much more sophisticated protection method, inspired by the last generation of disk protection, consists of writing erroneous data into the ECC (correction) portion of the data sectors. All CD-ROM players are equipped with electronics to correct this type of error, and the user is therefore not troubled by them. The 'track to track' copier is worse off since it loads this erroneous data, without difficulty, but writes it differently. So the copy doesn't work! This technique is typically used on the Sony Playstation console disks by exploiting the very high precision of the error detection systems of these machines. It's the prototype, therefore, of the almost totally copy-free disk for the moment!

All these mechanisms concern disks containing information data: CD-ROM, console disks. As for audio and video CDs, it's technically impossible to apply any kind of protection at the moment.

Be aware that the matter is quite different for DVDs which, it seems, use several already defined protection techniques, some closely linked to the hardware. For these, copying will certainly be much more complicated...

■ Recording without... copying!

The software which came with your recorder is designed for copying. Preparing the data is something you have to do in Chapter 7...

7 Preparation and set up

Prepare your PC and its software
Preparation of the hard disk
Configuring the recording tools

Before going on to recording proper, it's important to set up your machine. To evaluate performance, clean the hard disks... it only takes a few minutes. The objectives of this chapter are:

- to determine the fastest hard disk;
- to clean this hard disk to optimise its performance;
- with the help of this information, to select the optimal recording speed (1×, 2×, 4×);
- to configure the recorder buffers;
- to configure the software to prepare it for use.

■ Prepare your PC and its software

By performing these tasks, we will record in the best conditions, while reducing as far as possible the risk of spoilt copies due to errors of 'flow' and buffer saturation.

Choosing the best hard disk

Hard disk performance exercises a great influence on the fluidity of data. The faster the disk, the less risk of spoiling your CD-Rs. Consequently, the choice of disk is not something to hurry. Read any tests meticulously. They will help you to choose between the two recording options offered by the recording software:

- **File by file.** Using a file structure defined by your needs;
- **By ISO image.** That is to say, by first creating on your hard disk a complete copy of what your CD will be, then transmitting it whole to the CD-R.

Make your choice considering the following points:

- **Copying file by file requires a very fast hard disk.** A constant flow of data to the CD-R must be guaranteed.

Uninterrupted access to data in combination with real time CD-R creation is, in fact, a main source of time loss. In return, with this option, you need only several megabytes free to record your CDs.

- **File copying by ISO image is less demanding in terms of flow.** The work of formatting is already taken care of. But, to store a full CD, you must have at least 700 MB free space on the hard disk!

- **Consider the resources needed!** If you wish simultaneously to copy the contents of a CD to a disk (audio CD, video CD, CD-ROM disk), modify it, edit it, then re-copy it with an ISO image – you'll need 1.5 GB.

In conclusion. In the case of recording by files, you have no need to dedicate a disk to copying, but the disk must be very fast. In the case of the ISO image, the capacity of your disk is encumbered by the recording software. But disk speed is less important, and you eliminate the risk of flow errors. Fast disks have almost always a capacity of 1.5 GB, while smaller disks are slow.

The moral? To copy and record optimally, reserve a space of at least 700 MB and at best 1.5 GB on a fast disk, even if it means buying a new one!

That said, perhaps you are already the owner of several hard disks? In that case, choose the fastest, and reserve it. Nothing is stopping you from using it for other applications when you are not recording. You ought to take a few minutes to specify its name to the software!

■ Preparation of the hard disk

Once the working hard disk has been chosen, it must be prepared. If it's already full of files other than those necessary for the functioning of the recording package, create a temporary directory in the root. You can use it to store your working files: for example, D:>MESCD.

Be reassured, this directory has no effect on your future CD creation: the structure administered by the software is completely different from that present on the hard disk. You'll see anyway that it will be possible to shift files here and there into a multitude of directories, later creating a completely different file structure on the CD.

But first we must clean the disk. The two utilities we are going to use are accessible on the Start, Programs, Accessories, System Tools menu (see Figure 7.1).

- **First stage.** Disk cleaning and suppression of lost files using the ScanDisk command.
- **Second stage.** Defragmentation, that is restructuring of the disk's file system to speed things up. Start Disk Defragmenter. If you have never used it, your disk will probably be very fragmented, and the operation will be a long one. It might take minutes, or perhaps several hours.

Is it finished? We believe it useful here, to encourage you to install both commands, Disk Defragmenter and ScanDisk, directly into the Programs, StartUp folder of Windows 98's

Figure 7.1 It is very important to clean up your working hard disk before burning: a badly organised disk can cause many burning errors. Use system utilities such as Disk Defragmenter, shown here.

Start menu. They will thus be executed at each computer start-up and will only take, each time, a few seconds. Do not forget to point them to the proper hard disk, the one containing the working directory of your recorder.

■ Configuring the recording tools

Now is the time to deal with the final settings of the recording set up, before actual recording! Depending on the software you use, some programs suggest configurations and automatically recommend parameters.

Note! These configurations are not necessarily what works best. Two critical parameters are often suggested rather optimistically by the software: the buffers, and the default recording speed. But before coming to that, let's begin by telling the software to use the directories we set up for it.

Choice of paths
Your hard disk cleaned, it's perhaps time to tell your software how to use it. You have to change the 'default paths'. ISO images, temporary files, and 'layout' directories can be specified. By default, the software has probably located them on some undesired disks.

- Select Preferences in the File menu (see Figure 7.2).

- Set Temporary directories for files and Temporary directories for the musical cache to point to the directory which you created on the fastest hard disk (see page 90, Choosing the best hard disk).

- For software using the ISO image, such as Easy CD, specify also in the path preferences the path for your hard disk, and of the working directory (in our example, disk D:, directory MESCD). For those using other names (such as CD Creator) which describe the same function, set the 'recording buffer'.

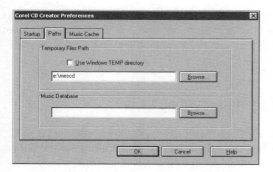

Figure 7.2 Configure your software to use the hard disk that you have just checked. You just need to indicate the correct path in the Preferences dialog.

Test the capacity of the set up

Now we must select the recording parameters. To set these ourselves, and thus to optimise those which the software chose for us, we must use all the available test facilities. It's long, it's tedious, but it's a guarantee of good results for our future efforts. The first stage is to analyse the configuration. In this example, we will use CD Creator. Do not worry if your software is different; it's probably supplied with similar options, accessible by the same sequence of menus.

In the File menu, select the System Test option. First select the option to test the hard disk. The software evaluates the speed of your chosen disk. The tested speed will be displayed (see Figure 7.3). It's to compare with the recording speed which you hope to achieve. A flow of 1600 KB/s, for example, will easily allow copying in mode X2 (300 KB/s). You can take it as a rule that the disk flowrate should be at least 2 to 3 times higher than that of the recorder. Now use the function Test Recorder. Prepare a blank disk. This will be requested by the recorder and the software (see Figure 7.4). Don't worry, it won't be recorded. The recorder then proceeds to try all

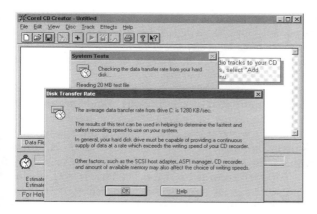

Figure 7.3 The software must evaluate the average speed of your hard disk to set the maximum recording speed it can use.

available speeds, while simultaneously reading some fictitious files which it will have created on the hard disk. The test permits the software to evaluate the precise speed that it deems permissible.

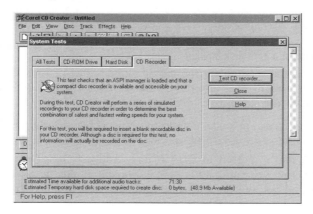

Figure 7.4 Evaluation of the recorder speed.

After testing the hard disk, the software can proceed to a test of the recording speeds permitted by the hardware. Careful: because your recorder is capable of 4×, this does not mean that the computer on which it's installed will be able to manage that capability. That is the point of this test.

This speed recommended by the software should not in itself be taken as an assurance of success. When the recording software simulates a write, it does not utilise all the possibilities of the system, far from it. A recommended mode X2 may work with CD-Rs on which you record 10 MB, but never on CD-Rs of 640 MB recorded in Mode 1! That is why, at the end of the software test, you should proceed to carry out your own test with the help of the function

 ### Recording simulation
All recorders are equipped with a Recording Simulation function. In this mode, supported by nearly all software, all the mechanical and logical devices of the apparatus are activated, as for a recording, except for the laser beam. The disk is therefore preserved. The advantage – you test recording in a real situation, and all the errors encountered can be resolved, without having to waste dozens of CD-R disks.

Simulation of a hard disk backup

We are going to simulate the recording of a disk of several hundred megabytes, using the default configuration recommended by the software.

- Start by creating a CD 'definition' (layout) by opening the File menu, Create Layout option.
- With the '+' button in CD-Creator (Add, or Drag-Drop with other software), add to the CD layout all the files you can find on your hard disk, to a total of 400 to 500 MB at least (see Figure 7.5).

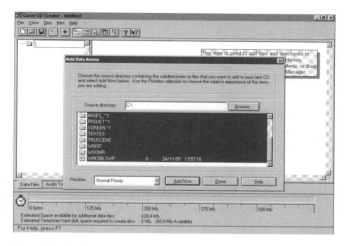

Figure 7.5 Simulation of copying a hard disk.

- Launch the option Record a CD from the file menu (Create CD from layout option).

- Leave all parameters as they are, but tick the Simulate recording option.

- Off we go, now just insert a blank CD and wait!

The best test

No test can ever replace an actual situation: the best possible test is always copying the contents of a hard disk on to CD-R. Here, your duplication set up will be tested to its limits, and in the exactly the same conditions you'll meet later.

Two possible solutions at the outcome of this test: the simulated recording ran correctly right to the end. All is well, keep the configuration. The other scenario, things went badly, say very badly: it's then likely that some 'buffer underrun error' messages were displayed. It will hence be necessary to affect some small changes.

Solutions:

- The most radical: lower the speed! Go from 2× to 1× or from 4× to 2×. It's a pity, that's life for you!

- Evidently, if you were already in Mode 1×, you cannot reduce anything. You must have a big problem! Insufficient active memory? Resident programs slowing things down? Examine all the global solutions possible to accelerate your PC.

But the most subtle solution, and the most satisfying, consists of changing the size of the buffers. Select the CD recorder Setup option, available in the File menu with CD Creator, and find the Buffers option (third tab in our CD Creator).

The read buffer is not very important, on the other hand, the one for writing determines the success of the operation (see Figure 7.6). Try to set it to the greatest size possible. Maximum buffer size depends on your recorder, and is probably listed in the documentation.

- Restart the recording simulation from the beginning.

- If all goes well, great, if it goes badly, hard luck, dear reader, but it will be necessary to lower the speed... or change your PC.

Overloading buffers

A simulation is no final guarantee of success! By changing the mode or the track format, buffer overloads may well re-occur. In this case, it will definitely be necessary to change to Mode 1× to resolve the problem.

Adjusting the buffers

Adjusting the buffers on the recorder is achieved via the recorder software menus (see Figure 7.6). The maximum

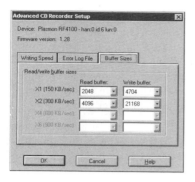

Figure 7.6 Buffer adjustment.

number of buffers allowed varies from one machine to another. Consult your documentation, and use all the buffers available.

Evaluating the CD-ROM player read performance

If you wish to use a CD-ROM player installed in the machine to make disk to disk copies, you must also test this. Start to test the performance of the player:

1. In the File menu, select the System test option.

2. First select the Test the CD-ROM option. The software evaluates the speed of the selected drive. You'll be advised of the test result, usually expressed in kilobytes per second.

3. Change the configuration of your recorder according to the result. 150 KB/s? Copying disk to disk will be impossible. 300 KB/s? You should be able to record in Mode 1×. 600 KB/s? You should be able to record in 2×. And so on. Note: CD-ROM players capable of a flowrate sufficient to record in copy mode with a 4× recorder are rare. With this recording hardware you should probably reduce your aims and restrict yourself, as far as copying disk to disk, to recording Mode 2×. Unless you buy a very good CD-ROM player.

Sensitivity and stability of the recorder

At last, we hope to draw your attention to the extreme sensitivity to shocks of some recording hardware. Some cannot sustain the least vibration. With some external machines, even a printer with a vibrating paper feed could be enough to interrupt a recording process! The recorder is a fragile machine that demands loving care and attention.

Briefly, internal machines aside, avoid at all costs locations exposed to strong vibrations and to temperature variation (radiator shelves). We won't even mention blows and savage shocks.

You have been warned... And if you abuse your CD writer, don't complain about having wasted a few disks!

8 Recording a CD-R: Preparation and planning

Preparing the disk for recording
Creating the layout

Everything set? Then now is the time to think of a CD-R recording of CD-ROM type. This is the basic application: record a CD-R containing an application intended to be read by any PC. This application could be:

■ multimedia software that you have invented;

■ a copy of all or part of a hard disk;

■ a copy of an application that you wish to distribute.

■ Preparing the disk for recording

We will not dwell here on the method used to create your application... let's say simply that somewhere on your PC resides an application that you want to record. A few practical hints will not be out of place.

Foresee what the user's machine will be

The first hint is to know the destination of your CD-R! Because the recipient must be able to read it it's therefore necessary to anticipate and manage future compatibility problems.

The author's personal experience

A book on recording doesn't write itself. It takes a little experience to be in a position to hand out good advice! In effect, manufacturers forget to deal with problems of distribution in the documentation that accompanies their machines!

I have accumulated a good number of multimedia CDs published in bookshops or distributed with magazines. The experience has taught me that the more the circulation of a disk is extended, the bigger the grind! And I know my subject! Up to now, around five hundred thousand industrial CDs have been recorded of my CD-Rs...

Disks for the press

You must be acquainted with cover CDs on magazines. Users faced with this very specific form of publishing will be rare. But the author can assure you that this type of 'mastering' is the most difficult of all! Imagine 100,000 users with 100,000 little foibles! It's truly necessary to 'stonewall', to foresee all eventualities, to stick to the standards at all cost!

The standard modes are known:

- Mode 1, monosession;
- file structure strictly ISO9660;
- applications designed for the flowrate of a CD player in mode 2× (300 KB/s).

Evidently, this CD is not the fastest and the flowrate is limited by the error correction protocol and Mode 2× does not allow full screen display of videos. But when you know the target, you must reach it at any price!

Conclusion: for very large runs, it's necessary to limit yourself to the most basic specifications possible. To record a CD-R which is readable everywhere, adopt Mode 1 (necessarily monosession), and the ISO9660 file structure (see Figure 8.1).

Disks using graphics and video

A CD-ROM of Father Christmas, in the shops for Christmas 1996, was the archetype of a CD-R having posed a multitude of problems. A brief resume of the scenario: a Father Christmas interactive, in video to AVI (Indeo 4) format, interacting with children via the mouse. Problems:

- At that time, the world was by and large full of 2× players
- The PCs were nearly all Pentium 90s.

The list of serious problems encountered with the masters was as follows:

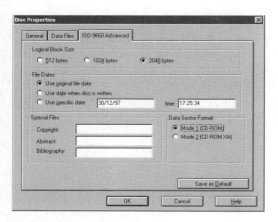

Figure 8.1 The CD-R standard!

- unreadable sounds;
- stalled videos;
- despairing slowness.

Here, you are at the heart of the wonderful world of multi-media and the hardware problems which go with it! The sound had been coded with too much precision for 2× players (22 kHz mode). It had to be reduced. The videos were not smooth enough, their flowrate had to be controlled, and limited to 150 KB/s. The slowness of the CDs was due to recording in Mode 1, with the praiseworthy aim of quality. It was necessary to record the disks in Mode 2 to suppress the error correction process that slowed the reading of the disks considerably.

Conclusion? For multimedia CDs, adopt the principle that your disks must be readable by the cheapest machines on the market.

On 20 March 1999, the ideal multimedia CD was running on Pentium II 350 PCs at the minimum, equipped with 8× players!

But the average PC is a Celeron 300 or a K6-300. Two generations late, but 80% of the installed market all the same.

This allows the exploitation of full screen video in MPEG mode without too many difficulties, of FM quality sound, and if need be to provide security on a track of data by adopting Mode 1 (to which the PC is less sensitive than an 8× or better still 16× player). Oh yes, the rich owners of fast machines will feel a little sore, they elected to go with MPEG II video, and CD quality sound, but everyone else will be able to use the disk!

Disks for encyclopaedia or software producers

The problem for the software producer is not properly speaking to the hardware. Here, the danger resides in the software already installed. An encyclopaedia user is likely to have his hard disk encumbered with a multitude of small bits of files, with drivers, already located by other software (Toolbook, Icon Author, Director) sometimes in an older version. It's the same with multimedia drivers: Direct X, Indeo (video drivers) for example, are already present, but in an older version, not compatible with your application. We do not have the space to develop this subject, but these instances will be the basis of another book. Let's just say here that it's necessary to foresee everything in the installation procedure included with a CD:

- reinstall all the video drivers, in the version corresponding to your application;

- reinstall all the drivers for the software producer in the version corresponding to your development utility.

Which brings us, logically, to the installation utility that you must add to your CD-R.

Procedure for creating an installation utility

Whether your CD is an archive or an application, if it's for distribution, it should convey a little touch of friendliness! So think about documenting it, that's the fundamental principle of installation. A simple 'readme.txt' or 'readme.doc' file is often sufficient to inform the recipient about the contents of the disk. For more sophisticated applications, an installation utility will be necessary. You'll find freeware versions of them on certain Internet servers:

- http://www.jumbo.com
- http://www.zdnet.com

■ Creating the layout

The first stage of creation consists in detailing a file structure. This is the layout, the arrangement of the directories on a CD. This is a virtual structure. It's used by the recording software to build the CD-R. But it does not correspond to the physical structure of the hard disk. It's made up of 'addresses', that is to say, of references which point to the 'true' files contained on the hard disk.

You therefore create your CD-R by opening a layout. This is often the Open new layout option of the software which starts the process. Once a layout is open, you fill it with files and directories:

- In Easy CD, add them using the Windows drag-and-drop feature.
- With CD Creator you take them one by one (see Figure 8.2), or use drag-and-drop.

Notice that the layout looks like a copy of a Windows 95 Explorer window. It represents what the CD-ROM will be. The layout, once finished, can be recorded on disk. It's not bulky, since it only contains 'pointers' to the files, and not the files themselves. It can be changed. You may add other files

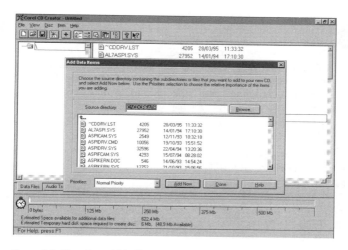

Figure 8.2 Choosing which files to copy.

or directories to it, and even replace some. For the moment, the layout corresponds to the format of your system: MS-DOS under Windows 3.0 or Joliet under Windows 95. Now we must define what format it will have on the CD.

Choose the file structure standard

In the majority of cases, the file system will be organised according to the ISO9660 standard. In this scenario, it will be exactly, or almost, limited to what you can do with a PC hard disk under DOS or Windows 3.0. You must therefore confine yourself to the following features:

- file names from the letters A to Z and digits from 0 to 9;
- sub-directories no more than 8 levels deep;
- name structures of ISO9660 type, say eight letter name, dot, three letter extension (nnnnnnnn.eee).

Be careful with ISO 'adapted' standards

Some recording software lets you record file structures of type ISO9660, 'adapted' for MS-DOS. To put it plainly, further to the ISO structure, they accept all the DOS special characters ($,# and so on). The ISO is or is not! If you choose a mode that is not perfectly standard, you risk finding yourself faced with compatibility problems. Always choose the 'true standards': ISO, MS-DOS, Joliet, according to the destination of your CD.

All the same, some scenarios justify the adoption of a standard other than ISO9660:

- If you use Windows 95 and 98, with up to date software, and therefore supporting the Joliet standard (programming, drawing, office tools software in the latest versions), it's possible that you'll have accessed files using the Joliet format. In this case, a CD recorded to the ISO standard will produce access path errors. In this case, you should favour Joliet.

- If your CD must work on both Mac and PC, the Joliet standard risks compatibility problems, and the Romeo standard runs the risk of not working if the file names are longer than thirty characters: therefore restrict yourself firmly to ISO9660 standard.

- If your CD must work under the widest possible range of platforms, DOS, Windows 3, Windows 95 or 98 and NT, for preference choose ISO9660 standard, which forestalls all risk of access path errors.

- As a general rule, the more widely a CD is distributed, the more preferable it is to use ISO9660 standard.

Quick note on ISO compliant naming standards

Before recording your CD, you must verify that no file with a Joliet name will be rendered unavailable by recording to ISO9660 standard. To make sure of this, in a DOS window type the command:

```
Dir *.* /S /P
```
and examine all the file names. If one of them is terminated by the characters such as '~1', it's possible it will cause access path errors and must therefore be checked further.

A Joliet future for file standard structures?

All these hints are only valid at the time of writing (March 1999). If ISO9660 remains the only universal standard, it's certainly necessary to add that the Joliet standard is much more friendly with its long names, that our PCs under Windows 95 or 98 use it, and that it's therefore much easier to record a disk with this format. In the coming months, the Joliet standard, as Microsoft has defined it, is going to become the standard file structure for all CDs. The progressive spread of the PC, of Windows 98, of Windows NT, and this system's adoption of long names for all new system software versions will reduce to virtually zero the risk of pathname errors and incompatibilities. You should therefore use the Joliet standard as the preferred one, and the ISO only if you really envisage that your CD-R will have to be read under Windows 3.x or MS-DOS.

Checking procedure

But, as we have said, adopting the Joliet standard is currently not recommended. It will not be read correctly by every PC, notably under DOS or Windows 3.x. Which therefore leaves only ISO9660 standard, strictly speaking. If, nevertheless, you have used Joliet to create your own disks, no problem should arise: your CD-R is a faithful image of your hard disk.

On the other hand, the ISO9660 standard poses three problems:

- It cannot accept the special DOS characters ('$' and '£' amongst others) which the recording software often replaces (without warning you) by '_'.

- It's limited to 8 levels of depth for subdirectories.
- If you use Windows 95, it truncates the end of file names by adding '~' followed by a digit.

You need to check the following points in your layout:

- No special characters/symbols, replaced by the symbol '_', these cause access path errors.
- There should be no names shortened by Windows 95 (recognisable by the name ending '~1') and if so, these files must not be referenced under a long name (Joliet standard) in an application or a description.
- No directory may contain more than 8 subdirectories.

 If you are copying a simple collection of files or working program, even a CD-ROM, these checks need not concern you.

Track optimisation

The layout is, in theory, recorded in file appearance order. In practice, it's possible to change this copy hierarchy. This is the notion of 'access time optimisation'. This optimisation refers to a simple principle: the disk, when read by a CD-ROM player, revolves permanently at constant speed. The disk being round, the outside edge revolves faster than the inside edge. A file stored at the outside edge is therefore loaded more quickly than a file located at the inside edge of the disk. This is a property which we are going to exploit to accelerate the loading of specific files: we will record at the start of the track, that is, at the outside edge. Simple, yes? For preference, this property is to be reserved for:

- video files;
- Wav sound data;
- programs which must be loaded quickly;
- as a general rule, whatever must be executed or loaded quickly.

How does that work? To optimise the speed of files, they must be given the attribute Fastest Access, or Faster Access. Thanks to these attributes, the files will be written according to their attributes, in the following order, starting at the outside of the disk:

- Fastest Access;
- Faster Access;
- All the other files.

With CD Creator, the Fastest Access or Faster Access property is defined when a file or directory is added: it's enough to select it at the bottom of the file selection box (see Figure 8.3).

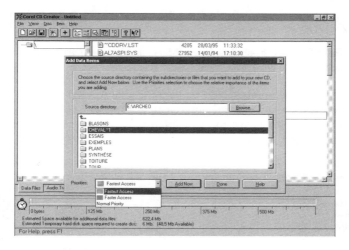

Figure 8.3 Speed optimisation options.

To add this attribute to a file or a directory contained in an existing layout, delete the file or directory to be accelerated and add it again to the layout, also giving it the desired attribute.

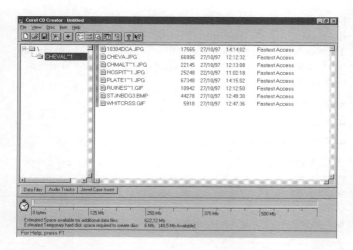

Figure 8.4 Once the attribute is set, observe the file acceleration colour markers in the file layout window.

In other programs, you'll be perhaps able to modify the file access attributes directly by opening a menu with the right mouse button, over the icon of the file or directory to be accelerated, and then validating the Fastest Access option.

Is it done? The accelerated file or directory is marked from now on with a colour symbol. Our disk is nearly ready.

To 'force' the location of a file at the outside edge

The menus for adding files to the layout of a future CD-R all offer possibilities for improving the speed. To achieve this they exploit the greater speed of the outside edge of the CD-ROM. To 'force' the location of a file at the edge just set the Faster Access attribute (CD Creator option).

9 Selecting recording software parameters

Recording software options
Protection while writing and recording...

We are ready to record a CD-R. What we now have to do is to configure the software using one of the innumerable modes available. Everything can be configured, the choice is up to you!

■ Recording software options

It's here that everything we have studied at the start of this book, concerning amongst other things the types and modes of the CD-ROM, is going to be applied. In fact, the creation of disk structure has nothing to do with the format of the disk. Briefly, we have a list of files and programs, we must now choose with which format the software is going to record them.

The file system

We have spoken in the preceding section about the file system. Here are the propositions which you must decide upon:

- All MS-DOS file names are valid. The file system is of 'MS-DOS' type, accepting the special characters (see page 109).

- Restriction to ISO9660 standard. The file system is strictly ISO. This is what we recommend.

- All Joliet file names are valid. The file system is compatible with Windows 95 and 98 and with long names.

Advanced ISO and data

ISO advanced mode will enable you to create 'documentation files' of the disk. These files consist of a copyright notice, another on the contents, and a bibliography index. These complementary bits of information are not strictly ISO, and we advise against using them other than in view of their use for an internal archiving system (for a business, for example).

- **Copyright.** Validates the presence in the system of a copyright notice.

- **Abstract.** Validates the presence of a notice on the disk.

- **Bibliography.** Validates the presence of a bibliography.

If, despite all, you adopt these options, you must provide the recording software with the file references (of type ASCII text, with extension .txt) containing the information (see Figure 9.1).

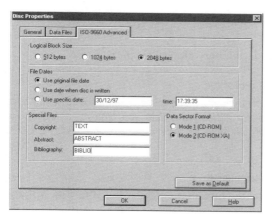

Figure 9.1 ISO advanced mode.

Avoid ISO advanced mode

ISO advanced mode is not necessarily compatible with a CD-ROM player and can seriously affect user access to your CD-R!

Dates

You can adopt various types of date for files to be recorded, independently of those already used by the system. Amongst the various options, you can:

Figure 9.2 Choosing a date.

- Use the original file dates (those of their creation or latest modification).

- Force the attribution of the date of writing to disk. It's the system time which is used, taken at the start of recording.

- Use your own date and time. You specify a time and date that suits you.

No recommendation here, do as you please!

Recording a prototype

To record a prototype, it's sometimes preferable to select 'Use specific date' for all files: the date and time of recording, for example. This will give an easy means of identifying a CD-R version.

Disk title and volume name

You can also enter information regarding the disk volume name and various references appropriate to software.

- **Disk title and artist name.** These details, often requested, are not reproduced on the disk. They are often used by the software to create sleeves for jewel cases (see Chapter 11 on this subject).

- **Volume label.** Only the first eleven characters are recognised and screened by MS-DOS or Windows. They represent the name displayed at the top of the screen when you type the command 'DIR'.

Here again, do as you please!

Block size

Most recording software programs authorise the modification of the size of blocks or sectors. Each track is, in fact, composed of blocks of a fixed size. The standard, as given in the *Yellow Book*, consists of blocks of 2,048 bytes in size. Software will often allow this standard size to be modified. The most current sizes are:

- 512 byte sectors;
- 1,024 byte sectors;
- 2,048 byte sectors.

This possibility to reduce the size of a sector is for the benefit of previous CD-Rs containing a multitude of small files below 2,048 bytes in size. It's becoming less current. It's an especially dangerous option, because platforms do not necessarily support sectors sized other than as defined in the *Yellow Book*.

In conclusion, therefore, always adopt a standard sector size of 2,048 bytes.

Figure 9.3 The optimum sector size.

Standard format sectors

The standard size of a sector is 2,048 bytes. Despite all the software options, always keep strictly to this size which is compatible with all computers and CD-ROM players.

Mode 1 or Mode 2

You can then record CD-Rs while adopting Mode 1 or 2. By default, most software programs record in Mode 1. The difference between Mode 1 and Mode 2 resides essentially in the possibility of supporting multisession mode (Mode 2), and in the inclusion of an error correction protocol (Mode 1). Please note that:

- The error correction protocol of Mode 1 reduces the space available for your data on the CD-R.

- Compared to Mode 2, the same protocol slows data transfer speed by some 20%.

- Mode 2 CDs have no error correction protocol, but today's players are reliable enough for its absence not to pose a problem.

Note, also, that only some rare and older CD-ROM players are compatible only with Mode 1. Nearly all players in our PCs are compatible with Mode 1 and Mode 2.

Briefly, let's say that:

- If you want to create a monosession disk readable by all the CD-ROM players on the market, you'll use Mode 1.

- If you want to make a hi-tech disk, compatible with any CD player fitted to a Pentium, a 486, or as a general rule, any PC sold since 1996, you'll use Mode 2. You heard me...

In conclusion: always adopt Mode 2, except for CDs which must be truly universal.

A few details on the XA standard

The XA standard is typically that of the multimedia PC: the synchronisation of sound tracks with information offers unsuspected development possibilities. In return, CDs corresponding to XA standard require that the player should be XA compatible. This compatibility consists in a set of microprocessors charged to decompress the sound tracks more quickly. At the time of writing, all the CD-ROM players in our PCs are XA compatible. Note that the reading of disks

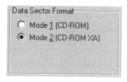

Figure 9.4 Mode 1 and Mode 2.

corresponding to the Kodak Photo-CD format implies the presence of a CD-ROM player compatible with XA standard.

As a general rule, software programs do not allow XA standard to be specified. They are content to attribute CD-ROM quality to Mode 1, and CD-ROM XA quality to Mode 2.

Software does not allow specification of XA standard

As a general rule, software will not allow XA standard to be specified. They settle for attributing CD-ROM quality to Mode 1, and CD-ROM XA quality to Mode 2. Mode 2 produces faster CDs than Mode 1 by dispensing with the error correction protocol.

Multisession or not

You'll not, generally speaking, have the possibility of selecting multisession mode. Your disk will be automatically multisession, from the moment when it starts recording in Mode 2. If you want to do a monosession recording (often the case), you can use Mode 2 and tick the box Protection against writing.

Monosession

Unlike Mode 2, Mode 1 is necessarily monosession.

What is the point of Mode 1, monosession? To add files to a previously recorded CD-R, and hence to utilise the maximum capacity. It's the first choice. Multisession mode is also used to make mixed CDs, that is, containing simultaneously digital information and audio CD. This is the principle of CD-Extra.

To arrange for a CD-ROM simultaneously to contain both information and music is not very complicated. Just make a first session containing sound tracks, followed by a second session containing digital data.

Sound tracks

An audio CD player necessarily reads the first session. The sound tracks must therefore be written in session 1 in order to be recognised.

To make a multisession CD with Easy CD Creator

Here is how to make a multisession CD with Easy CD Creator:

1. Write the first session in Mode 2, as if you were writing a data CD.

2. To add a new session, replace the disk in the recorder, and open the layout of the first session, or make a new one. Add the new files to the layout.

3. There are two ways to connect the new files to the previous session. For the first, select the option Load the previous session automatically. All the file tables of the previous session will be added to the new. For the second, less friendly, but more effective, load a session, which will display all the recorded sessions on the disk. You then only have to select the sessions to connect.

4. Start recording the disk.

To make a multisession CD with Easy CD Pro

To make a multisession CD with Easy CD Pro, follow these instructions:

1. Write your first session in Mode 2, but do not tick the Close disk box.

2. Save the layout.

3. To add a session, replace the disk in the recorder.

4. To replace the old data with the new, select the menu File, New, Multisession CD-ROM, and write the new session.

5. To connect a new session to an old, select the option Load the last complete track, if present. All the data which you add will then be connected to the old session.

6. Click on Record, that's all.

Recycling CD-Rs

If you 'recycle' CD-Rs by recording several sessions on them, do not forget that the old ones are not destroyed. Including... if you don't replace the file tables of the old sessions with the new... whatever you recorded in the old sessions will be accessible to the user to whom you give the re-recorded CD-R. And if this 'forgotten' data is confidential, that can be rather annoying...

Simple, multiple, and ISO image tracks

We still have to configure the write process. There are two possibilities:

- writing file by file on several tracks;
- writing all in one go on a single track.

As a general rule, it's writing all in one go on a single track that must be used: this is the ISO image notion (Easy CD Creator), or writing on a single track (the 'single track' mode of CD Creator). This mode has advantages and disadvantages:

- You need to make an image of the contents of the CD-ROM on the hard disk; the ISO image. It needs plenty of free space on the hard disk.

- The image having been made, the software can record it without further elaboration. The risk of error is therefore considerably reduced.

■ A CD recorded on a single track is very close to an industrial pressed CD and therefore of excellent quality.

■ Apart from creating the image, the recording process is very quick, and therefore perfectly suited to serial copying.

You can see that recording on a single track, or by ISO image, most definitely wins our approval. Even so, let's examine the track to track mode, or file by file.

■ No need to create an image in this mode, therefore the recording process starts immediately.

■ minimum. In general, 6 MB is enough.

■ Recording takes longer, the data flow is less well maintained, the risk of error is therefore higher.

■ The break-down into tracks takes up space, and the CD-R capacity is therefore reduced.

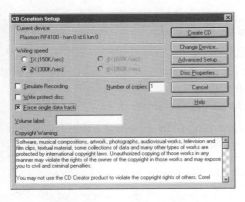

Figure 9.5 Choose the correct recording mode.

The scene is set, it's up to you, to look, to decide, to try! Are we ready to record? Yes, almost! Apart from a few details...

The correct recording mode

If the size of your hard disk allows it, use the Single Data Track mode, or ISO image, in the majority of cases (see Figure 9.5). It uses less space on the CD-R, and avoids a lot of recording errors.

■ Protection while writing and recording...

If you want to record the disk once and for all, click on Write protect disk, then no other session can be added afterwards.

If you want to avoid wasting CD-Rs, run a 'simulation recording'. The recorder verifies that the writing process will be error free. The operation does not change the CD-R, it remains blank.

As for the author, he willingly records without verification when he is pressed and someone else is buying the CD-Rs... And he verifies systematically when he is using his own disks! It's immoral! But human...

Everything is ready? All OK? Click on Create CD. In less than an hour, the job will be done!

10
Sounds useful

The audio CD conforms to standards and specifications just like a CD-ROM. These standards define the organisation of musical tracks, and the way in which their data is stored.

■ The problems of recording audio CDs

In a few words, music is stored on an audio CD according to the following specifications:

- The music is stored so it is readable in Mode 1×.
- The data on an audio CD is divided into blocks or sectors of 2,352 bytes.
- Each second of music takes up 176,400 bytes.
- Each sector is composed of 98 frames.
- Each frame is made up of 24 bytes of data, containing, amongst other things, six 'samples' of stereo coded in 16 bits.

Bored by all that? No panic, it was only for information! The only thing that interests us, is that the coded sound on an audio CD corresponds to a recording in 44 kHz 16-bit stereo mode. That's clearer? And yes, it's the optimal capture capacity for a PC with a sound card!

As to quantity, note also that you can record music to the limit of the CD duration (less a few megabytes reserved by the organisation system), and that the number of pieces will not be limited: 30, 40, 60? No problem, it's possible!

Armed with this information and a recorder, we will be able to make audio CDs by retrieving sound data:

- from an audio CD;
- contained in .wav files;
- from a sound source connected to the sound card of the PC.

In the last case, the sound source can as well be a vinyl record as an 8 mm tape, a DAT cassette, or any other form of sound source connected to the card.

What problems are there to solve when recording an audio CD?

- We should record a sound file of the best possible quality in order to benefit as much as possible from the potential of the media.

- If sounds are of poor quality, taken from a vinyl record, for example, we should improve them.

- We should retrieve and organise the sound files.

Noting all that, it only remains for us to study how to retrieve sounds, how to record the data, and how to listen to them (yet again, you probably know that already).

■ From one disk to another

The easiest copies are those that go from a CD to a CD-R. Sophisticated utilities, for some strange reason, are seldom capable of fulfilling such operations. With the exception of the Spin Doctor module, delivered with Easy CD Creator Deluxe.

Such a copy will nevertheless be possible by utilizing a track-to-track copying software program, such as CD Copier from Adaptec. The advantage of this utility: you have no need for CD players supporting digital extraction.

■ Audio CD, copied with Easy CD Creator

For more sophisticated copies, with track editing and organisation, it's more complex! The first important stage consists of retrieving some sound sequences. Several scenarios will present themselves: the options taken will depend on the form of the original source that we wish to reproduce.

 Note that one minute of recording takes up around 10 MB on the disk. It's not a good idea to reduce the file quality to save disk space: your ear would soon resent the poor sound from your CD player. Note the space then: 700 MB for a 70 minute disk.

Retrieval of the data

The mode of data retrieval varies according to origin.

From an audio CD

The retrieval of sound tracks from an audio CD has a name, Digital Extraction. It is really the digital retrieval of the sound data from a CD, as opposed to the analogue retrieval which takes place via a sound card.

Careful, not all CD-ROM players, nor all recorders, are capable of performing audio extraction. If your player is of this type, you are faced with the impossible, and would be well advised to change it for a more recent compatible piece of equipment.

Besides, not all software programs for making audio CDs necessarily have a digital extraction utility.

Come on! No panic, numerous freeware utilities are available. You can, amongst other things, download digital extraction software from the address

   http://www.tar dis.ed.ac.uk/~psyche/cdda/

The utilities offered at this address retrieve sound data and transform it into .wav files, which you can reuse later with specialised recording software such as Spin Doctor, delivered with Easy CD Creator Deluxe.

The CD Creator software, which we will use for this demonstration, allows audio data extraction without difficulty. It's

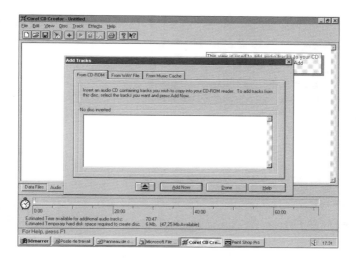

Figure 10.1 Extraction of audio tracks.

enough, when making the layout, to insert a disk in the player, specify adding a sequence ('+' button), and to extract. Note that the retrieved data will be copied into a 'musical cache', located on the hard disk, which must therefore be of a sufficient size.

The easiest means

The direct extraction of audio data from a CD is the most effective means of copying an audio CD while conserving the quality of the original. With CD Creator the operation is very simple: simply insert the disk into a Digital Extraction compatible player and add the track to the layout

From a peripheral connected to the sound card

The retrieval of data output from a sound card allows the capture of almost any sound. The contents of disks, cassettes, DAT tapes, and so on. To retrieve them, use the simplest utility in the world, Windows 95 standard recorder, or one of

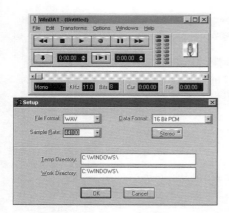

Figure 10.2 Choose the optimum digitisation settings.

the numerous shareware programs on the market (the one delivered with your sound card, for example).

Note: remember to record each sound sequence into a different file, otherwise you'll be unable to organise your tracks in your desired order.

The parameters for the quality of the retrieved sound will be the same as those for CD quality sound: 44 kHz, 16-bit, stereo (see Figure 10.2)

.wav File data

Existing .wav files can themselves be recorded without difficulty. No particular attention is required: the files are there already.

A greedy format

You are correct to digitise files in 44 kHz, 16-bit, stereo mode if you want to exploit all the possibilities of the audio CD. But this format is greedy for disk space.

Improving the data quality

The data now stored on your hard disk is not necessarily of good quality. Old disks, poor recordings means that the 'bugs' will not lack food. You can improve the quality with a sound editing utility. They are rather plentiful on the market. Some recommendations:

- Clicks and hisses are to be found located in the high frequencies. It's by working on this that you can reduce background noise.

- Loudness, which improves the 'spatial volume' of sound can be applied automatically to sound data by certain utilities, such as Turtle Tools. Don't forget to delete silences, which take up space uselessly. By default, recorders place pauses between tracks.

Preparing an audio CD layout

Are all your .wav files on the disk? The last step, the most important, is to prepare the layout. This consists in building a directory structure, as for a CD-ROM. The difference here is, we are not talking of a CD-ROM corresponding to the *Yellow Book*, with its ISO9660 system. In the case of an audio disk, it's a structure corresponding to the specifications of the *Red Book* that we are going to make: this will be readable and understandable by an audio CD player.

The first step, therefore, is to make a layout, exactly as for the CD-ROM. Here again, we will use CD Creator, but most of the other software utilities work in the same way with similar menu options.

- Click in the file menu on New CD layout, but this time, select the Audio Tracks tab (see Figure 10.3).

We must now record our tracks:

- Add your tracks to the disk by clicking on '+' each time: with the tab From CD audio to retrieve the track from a

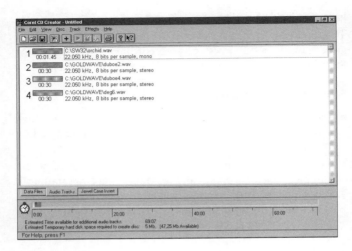

Figure 10.3 The audio CD layout.

CD that you'll have inserted into the player, and the From Wav file tab to retrieve a file recorded on the disk.

- The tracks are displayed in their order of reading. To change this order, using the mouse drag and drop the tracks from one window location to the other so as to obtain the desired order.

- To duplicate a piece, you can proceed by copy/paste.

- To listen to the content of a track, click on the Play button.

Is it ready? On with the recording!

Re-ordering

The layout of the audio CD contains all the tracks to be recorded on the CD-R. Here, the tracks in Wav format cohabit with tracks extracted directly. You may arrange your disk in any order you wish. This is ideal for managing the order of future 'compilations'!

Record then listen!

An audio CD recording should meet the *Red Book* specifications: Mode 1. To record the disk you have just put together, follow these steps:

- Stay in the layout window of the audio disk.

- In the file menu, select the Create a CD from layout option.

- In the CD Setup dialogue box, select the default options. No problem here, all the useless options are deactivated: Single Track and Disk Protection mode, for example.

- OK? We're off!

In a few minutes, you'll be able to listen to your disk! This solution is flexible and effective. There are others. In fact, for a long time, there was no simple and friendly software for making audio CDs. This particular operation certainly merited its own dedicated software however: a need filled by the 'Spin Doctor' module, delivered with Easy CD Creator these days. The advantage is that it resolves all the problems of sound duplication. It extracts or digitises sounds, embellishes them, and arranges them if need be, and then records the CD, almost automatically. What more could you ask for?

■ Recording a disk with Spin Doctor

Here you'll need a very good quality sound card (at least 16 bits). Recording will be quick: 30 seconds per minute of music on a 2× player, for example, with digital extraction.

The Spin Doctor interface, delivered with Easy CD Creator Deluxe, is remarkable. It breaks down into intuitive steps:

- **Step 1: choose Select Musical Source.** Vinyl record, cassette, CD, hard disk files (see Figure 10.4). Check that

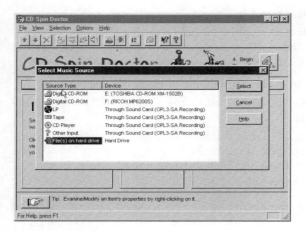

Figure 10.4 Spin Doctor, acquisition.

the source is of the best quality possible. In the event of acquisition, the results will vary according to the quality of the sound card. In any case, the objective should be to record while preserving the maximum fidelity of sound. No scratches and so on. Where needed, clean your vinyl records.

- **Step 2: select Recording Options.** It's here that the retrieval of sound begins (see Figure 10.5). It's here also that you'll apply certain quality improvement filters. Cleaning, loudness.

- **Step 3: choose Select Music Destination.** Storage on a hard disk for multiple and subsequent recordings, or immediate recording on a CD-R (see Figure 10.6).

- **Final step: record!** There is nothing more to do but wait... before listening! Admit that it's difficult to make things easier (see Figure 10.7).

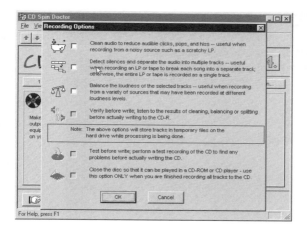

Figure 10.5 Spin Doctor, cleaning.

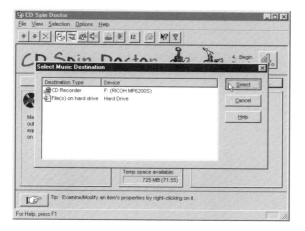

Figure 10.6 Spin Doctor, destination.

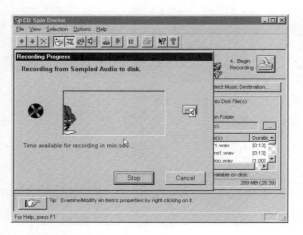

Figure 10.7 Spin Doctor, recording.

11
Problem
solving

Unexplained errors

If recording stops with a message

If your CD seems recorded but is unreadable

Got a problem? Tried everything, nothing left to do? That sounds bad, that's a show stopper, in short, it's a catastrophe. One chapter will therefore not be too much to try to diagnose the problems you meet. A few reminders about the rules to follow for solving your problems. To begin with the 'errors' while recording. They are nearly always due to a poor data transfer rate to the CD-R.

■ Unexplained errors

The CD-R recorder needs to receive data in a linear form and at the correct speed. In fact, it records data, with a very precise rhythm. If the cadence is changed or the flowrate irregular, recording will be stopped. Consequently, recording and disk will be lost.

The great majority of disk failures can be put down to a faulty data transfer rate between the hard disk and recorder. This is why the best recorders are those which are equipped with an internal hard disk.

For this reason, the slightest slowing down of the PC can be the cause of a recording breakdown, without the situation being marked elsewhere. These are the 'I don't understand it' types of breakdown.

Too many applications open at the same time
You are trying to work with an application while a recording is in progress. If this application, for whatever reason, accesses the hard disk or monopolises any resources (processor, DMA channels), it's possible that the PC will slow down overall. The speed becomes gradually inadequate, and therefore the recorder stops working for lack of data.

■ During a recording, try doing nothing else at the same time.

- If resident utilities are loaded, deactivate them.
- If software applications are running, close them.
- Stop all antivirus checks.

Windows 95 automatic operations

Your setup is equipped with Windows 95, and has just been working on an application which makes abundant calls on memory and the hard disk. A few minutes later, Windows will automatically erase all temporary and virtual files. Disk accesses will increase in an impromptu fashion and the data transfer rate will become inadequate.

- Try to arrange for Windows to be stable before starting recording, if need be by rebooting the computer.
- For your temporary recording files, try not to use the same disk as the one used for the Windows 95 swap file.

Incompatibilities with Windows 98

Strictly speaking, Windows 98 is not incompatible with recorders and their software, but several subtle modifications to the system and ATAPI drivers for IDE recorders which it installs automatically seem to pose problems in some cases, primarily with software:

- If you are using Adaptec software (Easy CD Creator) and you meet inexplicable problems, install the latest drivers from Adaptec (**www.adaptec.com**).
- If you are using WinOnCD OEM, and the software sometimes stops in the middle of a recording, ruining the CD-R, try to change to the new version 3.6.
- If you are using Nero and it cannot detect your recorder, try to install the patch or the latest updated driver from the recorder manufacturer. Possibly, try to change to Nero 4.

▪▪

■ If, in general, recording software does not detect your recorder after installing Windows 98, try to replace the Windows 98 ASPI driver by the one you will find on your CD.

SCSI recorders do not generally pose a problem with Windows 98. In case of malfunction, try to install the latest ASPI drivers from Adaptec or the manufacturer of your SCSI card.

Troubles due to a network card

Network cards consume a lot of processor power on some PCs. If the card becomes active, it's possible that, here again, the data transfer rate can be affected.

■ If the recorder is on a PC server, the processor power consumption is uncontrollable. Avoid this configuration at all costs. If necessary, suppress file and printer sharing while recording.

■ If your PC uses permanently active e-mail software, it can access a mail server at regular intervals. If the incoming mail is large, the disk can become encumbered. Solution: deactivate your e-mail software before recording.

■ If recording stops with a message

It sometimes happens that a recorder stops suddenly, the only explanation being a displayed error message. Unless you are lucky, it will not be very explicit. In many cases, it's still a data transfer rate problem that will confront us. And, perhaps, a faulty configuration. What a picture!

Problems stemming from the recorder

The recorder can create some problems connected to speed or the buffers.

Recording speed

Until recently, all CD-R recorders were of type '1×', that is, capable of recording at a speed of 150 KB/s. Then came '2×' recorders (300 KB/s) and '4×' (600 KB/s). The possessors of fast recorders are legitimately tempted to utilise the possibilities of their hardware. Unhappily this is a source of additional blackouts! The recording of CD-Rs being done in real time, each increase in speed increases the risk of seeing the data input flowrate to the recorder become too low. Don't forget that at 600 KB/s, the recording flowrate becomes very close to that of the hard disk, and the slightest incident then becomes catastrophic!

If you experience too many interruptions or recording errors, always start by reducing the recording speed to a minimum, that is, 1×; see the configuration table in Chapter 6.

Recorder buffers

The message 'buffers underrun' is typical of undersized or badly configured buffers. Set the buffers of your recorder to their maximum possible size, by reading your hardware documentation. If that is not enough, reduce the speed (see Figure 11.1). If this solution resolves your problems, it's probably a case of your machine not being capable of recording more quickly. Pity...

Figure 11.1 Reduce the speed

Problems stemming from the SCSI card

The SCSI card can engender problems of cable connections and of configuration.

Configuration

If the recording flow is erratic, or systematically interrupted, despite using a very powerful machine, your SCSI card is perhaps configured badly. Take another look at Chapters 4 and 5 and try to resolve any problems with old drivers which need updating. Check also, while you are about it, that the card parameters are adapted to CD recording.

Cable and terminator

SCSI chains are such that they can appear to be working correctly when in reality they are failing. However, inevitably, after a few minutes, a function rendered unavailable by the presence of a fault causes a recording error, of reading maybe or writing to the hard disk containing the data for recording. And without any explanation of any sort! On the face of it, it's illogical, in practice, it's that the SCSI chain is faulty. Check therefore that the cables are of good quality, that the terminator is installed, and the Terminator activated option of the SCSI card is validated.

Problems arising from a lack of hard disk speed

In many cases, you'll be able to resolve problems connected to the speed of the hard disk by increasing the size of the CD recorder buffers. The buffers, less frequently filled by large blocks of data, render the recorder less sensitive to the disk flowrate.

Inadequate speed

If you should use ISO image reading 'on the fly' or reading on an as and when needed basis from all the files, the hard disk must definitely be accessible at a speed slightly above the recharge rate of the CD recorder buffers. It's estimated that the average access time to data contained on the disk must be at least 19 milliseconds. Try to change the addresses of temporary files by pointing them, for example, to another hard disk.

Fragmentation

Disk fragmentation, this is the breaking up into a multitude of pieces of the files it contains. DOS, and also Windows 3 or Windows 95, are so conceived that new files occupy all the spaces left free after deletion of older files. Where necessary, breaking them down into small pieces. This fragmentation can slow the disk transfer rate a great deal. To control it, start the Defrag utility under Windows 3 and DOS (command C:>DEFRAG) or Disk Defragmenter, accessible from the Start menu, Programs, Accessories, System Tools (see Figure 11.2). If your disk is fragmented, start a defragmentation prior to recording a CD.

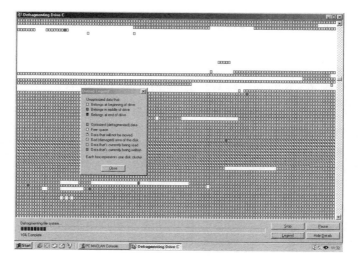

Figure 11.2 Check the fragmentation.

Thermal recalibration

Many hard disks make, at regular intervals, a 'thermal recalibration'. This operation allows the disk to ensure that its reading hardware is correctly controlled and that it will cause as few errors as possible. Problem: the recalibration blocks the working of the hard disk for a demi-second. If during this demi-second the recorder buffers were inadequately recharged, the recording process is annulled!

Some hard disks 'recalibrate' intelligently, waiting for all operations to finish: this is the case for disks from Micropolis and Fujitsu, amongst others.

■ If your CD seems recorded but is unreadable

Numerous imponderables can cause problems of reading.

Problems due to the choice of file structure format

Messages of the type 'unknown file' or 'missing file' are typical of an erroneous choice of file structure. You have not chosen an ISO standard, used Joliet or Romeo, and the PC does not support it. Try again with a typically ISO 9660 structure.

Problems linked to SCSI or IDE drivers

An ill-adapted SCSI or IDE driver (for example, an out of date version) might very well conduct a recording session right to the end, at the same time as peppering the disk with errors. Check that your SCSI drivers are really the most up to date versions.

The CD takes an interminable time to be read

This is typical of a badly recorded file structure or of an unreadable format. Check these two points. If the symptom still persists, try to record again in Mode 2 if the unreadable CD-R was in Mode 1, and in Mode 1 if the CD was in Mode 2. If this treatment works, be careful: your CD-ROM player is not perfectly compatible.

Problems related to SCSI or IDE drivers

An ill-adapted SCSI or IDE driver (for example an out of date version) can very well conduct a recording session right to the end, while totally destroying the CD-R! The CD-R is apparently OK. However, it doesn't work. In this scenario, typically, carefully check the SCSI chain and drivers.

Problems arising from the system

Bios versions succeed one another. An out of date Bios can be the origin of problems which are sometimes revealed following a CD-R recording. Check therefore that the Bios is not too old (see Figure 11.3). For that, consult the System option in the Control Panel.

Figure 11.3 Note the version of the system.

■■

Reading problems with CD players and consoles

The video-CD is not readable on a domestic player

You have probably recorded the wrong MPEG format or even a non compatible disk. Do not confuse video CD with a CD containing some video sequences: the video CD corresponds to the *White Book* standard. It's playable equally on PCs as on dedicated video CD players.

A CD-R can contain any kind of video (AVI, MPEG, Quicktime); it's playable on the machine for which it's designed (a PC in the case of an AVI file, a Mac or a PC in the case of a Quicktime file for example).

Only WinOnCD and Easy CD Creator can make true video CDs.

The video CD gives a flash on the domestic player and answers 'No disk' on the DVD player.

This problem was raised by a reader who had used the DVMPEG utility and recorded his disk with CD Creator.

In the event, it's probable that it's his compressor which was faulty: CD Creator, in its latest version, is delivered with XING, which is actually capable of generating an MPEG file playable in a CD-I player. It should not be forgotten also that domestic players absolutely must have video CD or video CD-I code to read a video. It's therefore imperative to use a software program capable of generating this code, and to follow its procedure step by step (on this subject read the chapter on making a video CD first). In every case, we recommend the strict use of CD Creator or WinOnCD.

The video CD is not read on a CD-I player

Careful: video CD consoles and CD-I consoles are different: some CD-I players need a cartridge to read video CDs, together with a suite of programs (CDI_Apps) which is not available in the shops.

My PSX disk copy is unreadable on my console

PSX disk copies are unreadable on a console because of their protection device. It needs a special processor, the modchip, to render the disk playable.

CD recorders seem quicker (access time and transfer rate) than CD-RW recorders: is this true? Would a 4× CD-RW be slower than a 4× CDR?

There is no technical difference between CD-RW and CD-R recorders; the explanation is commercial. All new recorders are at least 4× with CD-RW function as standard. They are therefore more efficient because newer, but a 4× recorder is equal to a 4× CD-RW recorder.

Questions and answers on CD-RW

Are CD-RWs as fast as CD-Rs for CDs and less quick for CD rewritables, or are CD-RWs slower for both types of disk?

A CD-RW disk can be slower than a CD-R because of its OSTA UDF file management system which takes up machine time. Otherwise, no difference!

Are CD-R-only recorders on the road to extinction?

Probably... The future belongs to CD-RW.

Having no real need for a CD-RW (except for DD backup, see below), do you think that I ought to be happy with a CD-R, or do you think that the price difference being minimal, for equal performance, it would be better to buy a more multipurpose CD-RW?

The functionality creates the need: when you have had a taste of this functionality, you can't do without it! Don't hesitate, buy a CD-RW, as these are quickly coming down to the price of CD-R-only recorders.

Can the CD-RW replace the ZIP drive to advantage: which is the quicker, the more friendly? Is it advisable to make regular backups of DD files to a CD-RW, or would it be so complex that it would be better to do it on a ZIP?

There is no difference in function between a Zip and a CD-RW. On the other hand, the Zip is much quicker than a CD-RW for the moment. On the price side, at £10 a unit, the CD-RW wins hands down! Making regular backups by CD-RW is perfectly feasible. What is dangerous, is to use a CD-RW 'on line' like a hard disk, because the limit of write/erase sequences can be reached rapidly.

In your book you say often that the best way to copy an audio CD is to use audio extraction. I am therefore obliged to put my disks into the recorder to extract their content. But doesn't using a recorder in this way (like a player) risk damaging the record head? Isn't it heavier than that of a player, and isn't one warned not to use it in this way?

Yes, the recorder head is heavy and its track to track access time slower. But no, using a recorder like a player is not dangerous for the recorder. It's a reader like any other. For example, one of my stations is equipped with a single recorder (Traxdata), which functions all the time in both modes (recorder and player) and gives absolutely no sign of faults.

Do you have any idea of the number of CDs that a recorder can record before encountering problems?

I can find very little information on the subject. Manufacturers speak of 'MTBF' or 'mean time before failure' which most often is stated in hours. In my view, it's possible to burn 5 to 10,000 CDs before meeting a problem, which will probably be connected, as with players, to head azimuth misalignment. By that time, the price of 40× recorders will be down to less than £50, so...

12
Post recording polishing

Stay on top

The CD is burnt, it works, all problems have been resolved: you are now in possession of a magnificent, brilliant and perfectly functional disk. The work is therefore almost finished. Almost? Yes! Because the software and hardware still have some surprises for us. Probably you doubt it's possible to write on the screen print of your virgin CD, but were you aware that you can also make jackets, labels, in short, render your CDs still more true-to-form? Recording software packages are often supplied with utilities for making jackets. To be used exclusively for classifying, tidying, organising (see Figure 12.1).

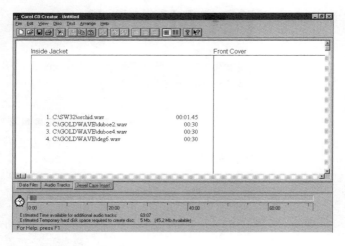

Figure 12.1 Improvements.

■ Stay on top

Regarding the disk screen print, there is little to say: you can write on it with a felt tip pen. Write the name, a version number and the recording date. That may be all that's needed:

CD-Rs have one thing in common, they all resemble each other, and when you have a large collection, you'll thank the author for this apparently flippant advice...

Keeping track of projects

There are other printing possibilities: the jacket, which you can later insert in the jewel case, for example, can be made with your software or by an accessory utility. This is the role of accessories such as Avery Media Software. This software is free and sent against the coupon you'll find in the pages advertising the brand.

For each part of a CD-R – the jewel case, the disk – Avery Media offers you a sample ready for use, to print on labels from the manufacturer.

The majority of software producers, notably WinonCD and Easy CD, also offer you their jacket management utilities, many of them unfortunately less sophisticated.

Some accessory products

You can also obtain from Inmac, Surcouf, and so on, a multitude of small easy to use products. From Inmac, for example, you can obtain colour boxes for CD-Rs, at the price of £5.50 per unit (a little dear all the same...).

Note that HP has a CD labelling kit, very practical, which consists of rows of labels ready for sticking, combined with a Labeler and a gadget for glueing. These labels can be printed in colour or in black and white by their own printers. The kit costs £35 and additional labels (sold in 30s) cost a little over £10.

ASpecialist software

Recording software

Physical copy utilities

Other utilities in old versions, and so on

Indispensable utilities

OSTA UDF software for rewritable disks

Author's privilege: he exploits and uses free of charge all the software kindly supplied to him by publishers. This allows me to present you with details of all the software currently available on the UK market, tested in their latest versions on 17 March 1999. Certain texts reproduced here have been published in *PC Magazine*.

■ Recording software

Initially let's examine recording software. At the moment, only three utilities are truly effective. We have tested them all before including them.

WinOnCD version 3.6

- Version tested: 3.6
- Publisher: CeQuadrat GmbH, Aachen, Germany
- Test configuration: PC 6x86 200, 32 MB RAM, hard disk 1.6 GB
- Environment: Windows 95/98, NT 3.51 and 4.0
- Address: http://www.cequadrat.com
- Drivers and compatibility:
  http://www.cequadrat.com/support/driver.html
- WinOnCD is delivered free with numerous recorders

WinOnCD is a particularly complete package: it allows the creation of video CDs to standard 2.0, of CD-Extra disks, of audio CD disks, ISO and CD-ROM. It extracts audio tracks without difficulty for all formats that the player and recorder can also extract. This software is the only one which incorporates an MPEG 1 compression utility directly in its video CD creation function: in short, everything is automatic, which is very handy.

It has an image track mode, supposed to allow the copying of disks, but this mode is particularly touchy for the less experienced to handle. To copy disks, here again, it's better to use WinOnCD together with a specialised utility such as CDRWIN (which is the author's software configuration). This mode has been replaced by the CD COPY utility inserted in this version.

The compatibility of WinOnCD version 3.6 with Windows 98 has been considerably improved.

Easy CD Creator Deluxe 3.5

- Version tested: 3.5
- Publisher: Adaptec
- Test configuration: PC 6x86 200, 32 MB RAM, hard disk 1.6 GB
- Environment: Windows 3.1x, 95/98, NT 3.51 and 4.0
- Address: **http://www.adaptec.com**
- Drivers and compatibility: **http://www.adaptec.com/support/overview/ecdc.html**
- No demonstration possible

A little miracle product incorporating all the experience of Adaptec over the years: first advantage of this software, the ASPI drivers which allow it to manage both IDE and SCSI recorders are the absolute market standard. Result? This software functions perfectly in all situations and recognises all hardware without difficulty.

Its strong points? It's one of the rare bundles (with WinOnCD) entirely dedicated to the creation of disks in video CD format, including CD-I applications. It's also the only one which includes the MPEG XING compressor (the best) and numerous functions for managing and manipulating MPEG files which make up the disks.

Here is the list of applications of this product to demonstrate that for less than £60 it's truly the one that performs best:

- Easy CD Creator for making CD-ROM disks;
- Picture CD Creator for making CD disks of photographs (not photo CDs);
- CD Spin Doctor for copying any audio source;
- Video CD Creator for making video CDs.

Nero 4.0

- Version tested: 3.0
- Publisher: Ahead
- Distributor: Inelec – Winshare
- Test configuration: PC 6x86 200, 32 MB RAM, hard disk 1.6 GB
- Environment: Windows 3.1x, 95/98, NT 3.51 and 4.0
- Price: £40
- Address: **http://www.ahead.de** / **www.wska.com**
- Driversand compatibility: **www.ahead.de/recorder.htm**
- Demonstration available on
  http://www.ahead.de/Demo.asp
  Valid each time with 2 month time limit

Do you want to record all formats, using every possible method of recording? For a small sum, Nero can do it: modes 1, 2, and XA, audio CD, mixed, HFS, bootable and even multisession with liaisons between sessions (for easier access to multiple sessions). What's included, Nero manages audio CDs perfectly: it can extract tracks and convert Wav files. The evolution of standards has been taken into account: it's possible to record file systems in all formats. So, you can use Joliet to record the long file names of Windows 95 and ISO modes 1 and 2 for ASCII or MS-DOS command sets. The interface, a layout window containing a tree of files to be recorded and tabbed menus for selecting recording options, is very friendly. The options are numerous and can handle all scenarios: ISO mode (with image retrieval from other software publishers for compatibility), recording on the fly or track by track, Mode 1× to 4× with optimisation of speed and files. It's all there!

The novelties of version 4 compared to previous versions are:

- full management of UDF format (to exploit CD-RW – rewritable disks);
- management of recording beyond 650 MB (Overburning);
- digital filters to improve the sound on audio CDs;
- label management utility;
- recording mode 8× supported.

■ Physical copy utilities

The physical copying utilities on the market are rather numerous, but one alone is truly remarkable: CDRWIN from Goldenhawk. It's mentioned many times in practical examples in this book.

Goldenhawk products

Goldenhawk products have the reputation of copying anything and everything. They are not creative tools, being tools for reproduction, but are very efficient! Just ask the owner of a PSX console what he thinks about it: nearly all know about the famous Snapshot! But it's time to get your notebook up to date. The new winner among copiers is not Snapshot (too complicated) but CDRWIN, which runs under Windows, and copies just as well as its glorious ancestor. Sold exclusively over the Web, this is the only drawback to these products which are – technically speaking – simply quality!

CDRWIN

- Version tested: 3.7 Beta
- Address: **http://www.goldenhawk.com**
- Price: £90
- Demonstration on:
  http://www.goldenhawk.com/download/
  functional in Mode 1×
- Drivers:
  http://www.goldenhawk.com/support/ide.htm
  gives you all the information for using an IDE recorder

CDRWIN was mentioned in nearly every paragraph dedicated to copying in Chapter 6. Running under Windows, simple to use, easily compatible with good IDE recorders (and all SCSI recorders), it's a tool limited to the bare minimum (a few buttons and menus), therefore easy to use.

The 3.7 beta version is available only to registered users. It retains the advanced functions of version 3.6. A new Backup Disk screen, simple to use, with all options listed on a single screen. You have only to select your peripheral and click Start to launch a copy or backup.

- The Extract Disk screen is redefined to allow easier copying of disks, tracks or sectors.
- The HP8100/8110 recorder is supported (it allows karaoke CD+G disks to be read).
- The configuration screen contains new options for configuring the use of the hard disks on your PC, notably for ISO backup images.

The new functions of CDRWIN 3.7 beta

Support for new recorders:

- Memorex CDRW-2216;

- Panasonic CW-7582;
- Plextor PX-R820T;
- Smart & Friendly 2224 Racer;
- Teac CD-R56S;
- Plextor 40Plex.

The 'backup engine' function for copying CD-ROMs has been completely rewritten to support copying disks with audio tracks and data organised in any order.

The CD-Text mode (to add titles and composers' names to audio CDs) is supported by the HP8100/8110 and SONY CRX100E and CRX110E recorders. The Plextor 40Plex will also support this function of reading and copying CD-Text disks. It's possible to make disk to disk copies with the recorders Panasonic 7502 and 7582 by upgrading the firmware for versions 1.17, 3.17 or 4.17.

Unfortunately the graphics editor is still not functional. Quite evidently, it's a question of a beta version with all the bugs that type of program can contain. If you find any faults, tell Jeff Arnolds about it: he will be most grateful!

Let's finish with a small comment: since its launch, CDRWIN has been downloaded one million times! Out of these, less than 1,000 copies have been registered. While acknowledging my complicity in this manifest theft, I cannot urge too much for CDRWIN users to register their copy: they will benefit from development plans and get higher recording modes (shareware being limited to Mode 1×).

Warning

Only use CDRWIN with Windows 95 if you have an IDE recorder, otherwise you risk compatibility problems.

IDE recorders recommended by CDRWIN (source: the author's site):

Model	Firmware
Hewlett Packard 7100, 7110, 7200	2.02
Philips CDD3610	2.02
Memorex CRW-1622	D3.6
Ricoh MP6200A	2.03 or 2.20
Traxdata CDRW2260 Plus	2.02
Wearnes CDRW-622	D3.6
Yamaha CDR401	1.0j
Yamaha CRW4001	1.0d

DAO and Snapshot

- Address: **http://www.goldenhawk.com**
- Demonstration on:
  http://www.goldenhawk.com/download/
- Drivers:
  http://www.goldenhawk.com/support/ide.htm
  gives you all information for using an IDE recorder

DAO and Snapshot are the DOS ancestors of CDRWIN: efficient tools for copying, but unfortunately outdated. They are really too complicated to use.

Despite everything, you can download them at the address below, if only for the benefit of all the small users who need the performance of a multitude of tests on CD recorders and players.

PSX Backup together with DAO

- Address: http://www.goldenhawk.com

PSX Backup is a utility (not free) that controls the DAO copy software program and its utility CDCLIP. It's in a way a friendly interface for Snapshot under Windows, which aids easier track copying (and which also adopts configurations which allow certain protection devices like audio tracks of four seconds to be overcome). In fact, the real problem with PSX Backup, is that it's in German (as is their site). This small aggravation aside, PSX Backup is truly the best means of using DAO and Snapshot.

The Gear range

- Address: http://www.elektroson.com
- Price: £90
- Demonstration available mainly on: http://www.hyperdrive.com/gear/index.html#sweet
- Drivers: most IDE/SCSI recorders supported. You can download a generic drive at the address: ftp://ftp.elektroson.com/pub/windows/win95nt/gen_recorder_update/recorder_update.exe

The range of Gear tools is not very well known, although well conceived and capable of making numerous types of recordings. Gear arose out of Unix, for which it was created to serve the duplication industry. It's supplied for Windows with a very friendly user interface. The strong point of Gear tools are:

- system created for industrial duplication and hence of very high reliability;
- high speed;
- highly simplified interface;

- professional pre-mastering tools, ideal for generating disks ready for recording on Glass Master;

- supports recording robots over small runs.

The range is divided into several applications.

CD-R Suite

The three utilities which compose the Gear range, regrouped into a single package, are:

- Replicator;

- Gear Audio (copying from CD disks, vinyls and existing audio sources);

- Webgrabber, tool for copying a Web site on to a CD-ROM.

Let's examine these products separately, leaving out Webgrabber which is a highly specialised application.

Replicator 1.2

Replicator is a recording software program reduced to its most simple form: an assistant for Windows 95 and NT 4.0, which allows the creation of a copy of most CD-ROMs on the market, of video CDs, and of audio disks.

The procedure is simple:

1. Insert an original disk.
2. Select the temporary storage option.
3. Read the contents.
4. Insert a blank disk.

Difficult to make it more friendly! In fact, Replicator draws inspiration from the concept of CDRWIN. Without approaching its level of exhaustiveness (Replicator fails when it comes across certain protection devices such as four second audio tracks), nevertheless it copies 90% of the disks on the market!

Gear Audio 1.0

Gear Audio is a copying tool for all audio sources. Advantage: its filters allow it to suppress clicks and other aural problems, which is ideal for copying from vinyl records.

The interface is friendly, and it's possible to modify the properties of a sound or of a sound passage, to improve them, for example, directly from the software.

Gear Windows 4.3

Gear Windows 4.3 is a tool designed for recording CDs under Windows 95 or NT 4.0. It's less greedy with machine resources: this is its advantage; it's rather frugal and not extensive: this is its disadvantage. Up to today, it's still not sold for Windows 98, which is rather a bad sign!

CD Audio Creator

- Audio CD-R creation tool
- Version: 1.0
- Publisher: Micro Application – Data Becker
- Distributor: Micro Application
- Test configuration: PC 6x86 200, 32 MB RAM, hard disk 1.6 GB
- Environment: Windows 95/98
- Price: £21 approximately

CD Audio Creator is a very fine tool for your recorder. What is it used for? To record very nearly any sound source in audio CD form! It's the ideal tool for retrieving data from a vinyl record, an audio cassette, or again from a sound card. The program has all functions required for manipulating and managing analogue sounds: elimination of bugs, certainly, but also a whole range of effects, and some amusing options such as the 'medley' button.

Disadvantages? The sound must be stored on the hard disk, and an audio CD takes up room: in all, nearly 700 MB! Neither you nor the software can change that, it's the constraint inherent in digital audio sound. The list of recorders supported is not very long to look at, but by the set of OEMs, the majority of IDE and SCSI recorders on the market will be supported.

■ Other utilities in old versions and so on

These other tools are perhaps forgotten products, or obsolete software maybe! If any of them form part of your recording setup, we strongly recommend you to combine them with one of the software programs listed or request an updated version from your supplier.

Easy CD Creator 3.0

- Version tested: 3.01D
- Publisher: Adaptec
- Test configuration: PC 6x86 200, 32 MB RAM, 1.6 GB hard disk
- Environment: Windows 3.1x, 95, NT 3.51 and 4.0
- Address: **http://www.adaptec.com**
- Drivers and compatibility: **http://www.adaptec.com/support/overview/ecdc.html**
- No demonstration possible

In 1998 it was the most complete and sophisticated software on the market. It remains so, and it's one of the rare tools you can buy second hand.

Nero 3.0

- Version tested: 3.0
- Publisher: Ahead
- Distributor: Inelec – Winshare
- Test configuration: PC 6x86 200, 32 MB RAM, 1.6 GB hard disk
- Environment: Windows 3.1x, 95, NT 3.51 and 4.0
- Price: £40 approximately
- Address: http://www.ahead.de
- Drivers and compatibility: www.ahead.de/recorder.htm
- Demonstration available on:
  http://www.ahead.de/Demo.asp
  Valid each time with a 2 months' time limit (example: downloaded 19 Aug 1998, valid until 31 Oct 1998).

This version is obsolete. It's not very suitable for audio CD recording, as opposed to the following version, 4.0, which supports mode 8× as standard.

Nero version 3.0.5.0

- Address: http://www.ahead.de/Presse.htm
- Price: $999 (with the recorder...)
- Drivers and compatibility: delivered as part of a bundle with the That's Write recording software.

This version of Nero is a Package delivered exclusively bundled with the That's Write Fast X 820S recorder. The only 8× recorder which was a true and spectacular novelty in 1998 has become a total 'has been' in 1999! In fact, this year, all the new models are out in mode 6× or even 8×. Ahead, who are well aware of this, have integrated this mode as standard in Nero 4.

WinOnCD OEM version

- Version tested: 3.5
- Publisher: CeQuadrat, Aachen, Germany
- Test configuration: PC 6x86 200, 32 MB RAM, 1.6 GB hard disk;
- Environment: Windows 3.1x, 95, NT 3.51 and 4.0;
- Address: **http://www.cequadrat.com**
- Driverand compatibility: **http://www.cequadrat.com/support/driver.html**
- No demonstration available: WinOnCD is delivered free with numerous recorders.

This version of the software is currently replaced by the 3.6 version which we described above. You'll not find it in the shops any more. Note that it's rather poorly integrated to Windows 98. If you must use your recording software with a station equipped with the latest version of Windows, opt instead for the latest version 3.6, which you can order directly from CeQuadrat.

CD Right!

- Version tested: 1.5 / French
- Publisher: Prassi;
- Distributor: Site Internet
- Address: **http://www.prassi.com**
- Environment: Windows 3.1x, 95, NT 3.51 and 4.0
- Models: only copy, audio CD.

CD Right! has one big fault: Prassi have lost a case against Adaptec, and their software is now officially withdrawn from sale. It's a good bet that it will never be updated...

Padus DiskJuggler

- Address: http://www.infinitytec.com/
- Version: 1.01.199
- Price: £40 approximately

Demonstration on:
> http://www.infinitytec.com/infinity/padus/
> Padushome.html

This is old software, still sold, not widely available. It evolved little, but it evolved nevertheless... Its big advantage is that it has no difficulty copying four second tracks (very fashionable protection device). In view of this, it might be interesting to download the demonstration, limited to Mode 1×, which sometimes allows certain copying problems to be resolved.

■ Indispensable utilities

You'll sometimes need a certain number of utilities to perform specific operations, notably audio extraction, which will turn you into a magician if your hardware is not 100% compatible.

This is the address where you can find the most utilities for managing mode CDDA:

> http://www.tardis.ed.ac.uk/~psyche/cdda/
> CDDAsoftware_f.shtml

Some are freeware, others shareware. Here is a selection from the best of these utilities.

CDDA Extractor 0.91

A rudimentary utility interface, but one precious ability, the extraction of audio data via the ASPI interface: shareware without restrictions which you must own (and register!).

Audiograbber v1.20

A new extraction tool, which reads DA data via the MSCDEX interface (and soon via ASPI). A beautiful interface with large buttons for the shortsighted!

CDDA

The top, very well known and successor to DA2WAV for 32 bit Windows. Works in DOS command mode, but with flexibility; it's above all capable of reading across all interfaces (ASPI, MSCDEX).

Another practical tool, ASPICHK (by downloading from Adaptec), which checks the quality of your drivers, including ASPI and IDE. Arm yourself also with PC station performance evaluation tools: some, such as 'speedometer', are delivered with the Traxdata recorder, or downloaded from software publisher sites or sites of hardware manufacturers. These tools are practical, because they allow you to determine exactly the maximum speed at which your recorder can make CD-Rs in complete safety.

■ OSTA UDF software for rewritable disks

Spelt out, OSTA UDF is the Optical Storage Technical Association for a Universal Disk Format. This standard is to rewritable disks what MS-DOS was to our diskettes: a file management system. It allows CD-RWs to be organised, which, exploited in the same way as the CD-R, would only receive fixed data, in the form of accessible disks like a diskette. The current version of OSTA UDF is the 1.5 and corresponds to ISO 13346 standard. There are several free utilities which allow CD-RWs written in OSTA UDF mode to be read: it's very practical for example to transmit a CD-RW to a correspondent and simultaneously send him the OSTA driver which allows him to read his disk. Get it from Adaptec at the following address:

**http://www.adaptec.com/products/overview/
udfreaders.html**

and so obtain all the necessary OSTA UDF drivers free. And how does one record in UDF one asks? Good question! Quadrat offers its writing software Packet CD, at a very good price, and Nero includes OSTA UDF mode as a standard since its last version. At Adaptec, it is Direct CD that looks after making this type of disks.

Index

....